GAME TIME

GAME TIME
INSIDE COLLEGE FOOTBALL

TED A. KLUCK

THE LYONS PRESS
GUILFORD, CT
AN IMPRINT OF THE GLOBE PEQUOT PRESS

The Lyons Press is an imprint of The Globe Pequot Press.

10 9 8 7 6 5 4 3 2 1

Printed in the United States of America

Designed by Kim Burdick

ISBN 978-1-59921-199-2

Library of Congress Cataloging-in-Publication Data is available on file.

For Tristan.
May you never make an idol of football.
It's just a game.

CONTENTS

ACKNOWLEDGMENTS

Special thanks to Scott Rex at Central Michigan for the great access to practices and the Pro Day, ditto for Bob Kubiak at Olivet College, Ted Bowers at Taylor University, John Maurer at Rutgers, Vic Knight at the Senior Bowl, Justin VanFulpen at Verius Football, and all of the kind folks at Phil Steele's office in Cleveland.

To Herb Haygood for being a great teammate, to Max Pollock for going to class and generally raising the bar for student-athletes everywhere, to Mark Hagen for showing my dad and me around at IU in 1994, to Dan Bazuin for being a class act and for a great interview, to Danny Wuerffel for using your life and your celebrity to make a difference, and to Charlie "Mad Dog" Thornhill for showing me the "Game of the Century" and a great evening of conversation. May you rest in peace my friend.

Finally, to Josh Rosenberg, Tom McCarthy, and the rest of the team at Lyons Press for all of the help.

INTRODUCTION

A GOOD FRIEND of mine once wrote to me: "I long for the unleashing of real Truth that proves itself by changing people's lives for the better. But what I do feel deeply is that life is too short to read things that aren't marked by beauty, that don't somehow give life like a gush of cold water in the mouth of the person who reads. I feel like you'll understand this because of the 'Zen' (to quote an old Jazz instructor) of *Facing Tyson*."

It's 12:06 A.M. on the night before my deadline, and I'm still trying to find the beauty, or the Zen, in this book. Beauty is tougher to find in football than it is in, say, boxing, which was the subject of my first book. You can't help but run up against it in boxing with its collection of lovable and honest misfits. But it's tougher here. Men better than I have written about things like crisp fall days, bands, great teams, and the like. I won't try to wax poetic about the college game because I can't, and because I just don't see it here.

This book has given me another experience, which is the pit-of-the-stomach fear that perhaps I shouldn't have written it. That perhaps I was "mailing it in," so to speak. That maybe I don't have enough big names attached because big names sell books. But then I realized that there is truth and beauty in college football. Football is about defending lines. It's about objectivity. It's about people who Made It and people who didn't, and I had the privilege of writing about both types on these pages.

I remember the night well that I fell in love with the college game. I was eight years old and the Penn State Nittany Lions— they of the already archaic coach Joe Paterno and the vanilla uniforms—were playing in the Orange Bowl against the University of Miami, their camouflage pants and already considerable swagger. Being a humble Midwesterner, my dad had already taught me that we were to root for Penn State, slow white linebackers and solid old-fashioned values, as opposed to the bling-bling and bombast of the 'Canes. He let me stay up late that night and watch as the Penn State defense frustrated and dismantled the vaunted Miami "O" en route to a national title.

Fast-forward ten years, to 1994. I am a high school senior and a marginal college recruit, but I've been invited by Indiana University to tour the football facility with my father and meet the coaching staff. We are walked onto the Astroturf at Memorial Stadium and shown the rows of gleaming crimson and cream helmets—one of which could be mine. We are walked through the acres of weight room, the athlete's dining hall, and finally led into a theater where we are laden with recruiting materials and shown a highlight film. It is one of my proudest moments as a son, though I would choose not to play there, which I still regret.

As I type these words, we have seen a week (during the 2006 season) in which an on-field brawl turned a college football game in Miami into a street fight in Miami, complete with head-stomping and the swinging of blunt objects. We saw a pro player, Albert Haynesworth, suspended for stomping on the unhelmeted head of an opponent. We saw the line walked between sport, entertainment, and unbridled chaos.

As I type this, All-World running back and endorser of products Reggie Bush may be forced to give up his Heisman Trophy for allegedly allowing his family to receive hundreds of thousands of dollars worth of inducements from a potential agent. Bush is unmoved by the whole affair, as he is playing the role of post-Katrina Savior of New Orleans, and making millions the legitimate way as an NFL rookie. Rhett Bomar, a promising young quarterback from Oklahoma, is currently serving a one-year suspension for taking money from a booster, and will reportedly be exiled to a dusty football outpost called Sam Houston State to finish his career. And this season's Heisman winner, Troy Smith from Ohio State, has had his résumé marred by his own brush with an unscrupulous booster a few years ago.

And it seems like pro football is now what happens in between officials' conferences, roughing the passer penalties, and instant-replay reviews. And it also feels like besides perennial bottom-dwellers such as the Lions, Cardinals, and Raiders, every other team in the league is either 8–8 or 7–9. Feel the excitement. It has also always been strange to me that in the NFL, after a team gets destroyed by a rival, the majority of the players can bounce out to midfield and throw their arms around their opponents— chatting, no doubt, about wives, children, their fast-food franchises, and offshore bank accounts. It is as if they're telling us, "Although we got pounded today, we all make more money than you will ever see in your lifetime. There are no real losers here."

Thus, our ongoing need for college football. Because as long as there is college football there will be walk-ons, like Michigan's Max Pollock, who is an honor student and the son of Harvard grads. There will also be small colleges, like Taylor University and the University of Saint Francis, where football really is an extracurricular activity and not an excuse to throw major donor cocktail parties and sell stadium suites.

And for every narcotics bust, academic nonqualifier, and recruiting violation, there are handfuls of players like Central Michigan All-American Dan Bazuin, who in spite of their excellence on the field seem to have a firm grasp on their place in the grand scheme of things. There are recruiters who have retained a sense of ethics, like Mark Hagen at Purdue; and there are coaches who used to be stars, like Herb Haygood at Olivet College. And there are legions of coaches, like Taylor's James Bell, who are struggling to hang on and win at what may be the end of the line.

My goal was to blend equal parts of my first two Lyons Press titles—the journalistic (*Facing Tyson*) and the participatory (*Paper Tiger*)—to take the reader inside college football. At some levels I think I succeeded—I think the Pro Day and Senior Bowl chapters worked especially well—but this was by far my most meandering and disjointed project to date, as I found that interviews with college kids are, at best, hit or miss. The book also has a decidedly Michigan and Midwest-centric feel, as I learned the hard way that flying halfway across the country to interview a college student who stared at the floor and mumbled halfheartedly through his answers was not necessarily worth the money. The book is also pro-oriented, in that much of it deals with the NFL Draft, agents, scouting, and the passage from college to professional player via the Senior Bowl and Pro Day chapters.

But perhaps the most interesting and beautiful passage, to me, is that transition from college football player to former football player. It's one of the hardest transitions I've ever had to make, but I have the utmost respect for the men who make it well. This book is for them.

CHAPTER 1

THE HOLY WAR:

JAMES BELL AND TAYLOR UNIVERSITY VERSUS UNIVERSITY OF ST. FRANCIS

DRIVING ON TO CAMPUS at Taylor University for the first time since I was there as a player I am immediately reminded of the de facto caste system in place, as scores of beautifully scrubbed, well-to-do students and alumni pour out of the Rediger chapel/auditorium.

There were girls on campus with the same names as some of the buildings. It was just a small part of my education—learning that girls with dads and grandfathers who have buildings named after them don't want to go out with guys from small towns who drive rusty pickup trucks. But as this is a beautiful Indiana fall day, and as the beautiful people swirl around me, I choose to be positive, and give this place the benefit of the doubt again because there is much to love.

Curving around the circle drive, past the Rupp Communication Arts Building where I watched countless screenings of *The Breakfast Club* and wrote countless reaction papers about my feelings, I pull onto a gravel road that leads to the old, gray, football field house.

With just over 1,800 students enrolled, and more women than guys, the football team really is the school's best shot at any real socioeconomic diversity on campus. We all discovered it together back then, lots of blue-collar small-town Indiana kids who grew up in towns like Elwood, Tipton, and Hartford City. We discovered that for the first time in our lives we were in the minority, even though, like us, the majority of the campus was white. The realization starts almost the moment one wheels a car into a dormitory parking lot, to find that the freshman girls drive nicer cars than our parents do.

I always felt a special burden for the black players too, of which there were never more than a handful in any given year. It is with interest then that I flipped through an alumni magazine to see that Taylor had hired James Bell, a black coach who was last at Jackson State.

I am blasted by the Indiana wind that rips through the flat campus each afternoon as I enter the Field House, which looks and smells exactly like it did ten years ago. The marriage of football and Christianity is odd here, and I've always been intrigued by it, even as a player. Football is a violent game, and doesn't seem to jive with a campus where Biblical Literature and Foundations of Christian Thought are prerequisites for every student. I peek my head into the weight room, with the purple and gold paint on the walls, and the same cheap motivational slogans that appear in every weight room in every university in the United States.

James Bell doesn't turn around when I rap my knuckles on his open office door, as he is working on his computer. This doesn't exactly fill me with confidence. The fact is, I am still afraid of football coaches. It's residual fear, left over from years as a player, and the fact that back in those days these guys could ruin your life with a look, a phrase, or a chirp of the whistle.

Perhaps part of the reason for Bell's mood is the fact that he is trying to prepare his team (0–11 the previous season) to face the undefeated St. Francis Cougars, an upstart NAIA program filled with former NCAA Division I nonqualifiers and blue-chip recruits. The Cougars are a small-school juggernaut with appearances in the last two NAIA national championship games under their belt. They beat Taylor 55–0 last year, and 46–0 the year before that. And the start has been rocky this season as well, with a win over Greenville College bookended by losses to Anderson, Quincy, Urbana, and Walsh.

I can tell that building rapport here will take some doing, as coaches who have been in the business as long as Bell has have built up a latent distrust for those in the media. I will attempt to communicate that I am, hopefully, something other than "the media."

There aren't many black faces in Upland, Indiana. I begin by asking Bell how his experience has been. Not surprisingly, he says that it's been positive.

"More than anything it's the leadership here," he says. "With [president] Dr. Habecker here. Wanting to do things right. It's his heart.

"Winning here is similar to some other highly academic schools I've been involved with, like a Wake Forest where you need eleven hundred on the SATs just to get in here," he says, when I ask him what it's like to build a football program at a place where religious and academic standards are so high. "Not only are you battling the academics, but also you're battling a stigma . . . the

stigma of 'they can't do it' or 'it can't work.' You do what you do because you are supposed to. Because it's the right thing to do."

Bell speaks often about the right thing. He has wheeled his
chair back from the computer, which is a good sign, although he
still looks down at me over a pair of half-eye spectacles, which I
find an odd choice for a football coach. He is of middle age and
looks not unlike a more distinguished Billy D. Williams in some
lights. The office is orderly. Everything has a place. A pile of la-
beled videotapes in one corner. A stack of coaching magazines.
Two Taylor helmets—a purple model, and the newly updated gold
that the team will wear this season. Walking down the hall to get
to his office, I passed the open door of another coach, who was
feverishly breaking down game film. These are things one would
see happening at a Division I program; it just happens here on a
much smaller scale.

"I think it's been a smooth transition," he says of moving his
family into a predominantly white community. "Everybody has
been very helpful. Very cordial. They have been supplying the information you need. Where to fix your car. How to deal with aca-
demia. That's what you want, and what you work for. People
constantly ask me why I came to Taylor . . . and it's because it's
just the right fit. I'm comfortable with them, and they're comfortable with me. That's the bottom line. I'm not saying that's right or
wrong . . . but that's just the way it is."

In decades past, Taylor played in the less competitive NCAA
Division III, where its opponents were largely private, academic
schools and, more important, the doling out of scholarship monies
was prohibited. At least by appearances, all of the schools stood on
equal footing. In the early 1990s, however, Taylor moved to the
NAIA, where scholarships are allowed, and found the going much
tougher.

We are interrupted briefly, when one of my old assistant
coaches comes to the door. He is a holdover from the old regime,

as Bell only brought a couple of "his" guys to the staff. This is an awkward transition with any new hire. Does the coach "clean house" and stock the cupboards with his guys, or is there some overlap in regimes? We exchange greetings, and Bell gets up from his chair to close the door on any further interruptions.

"For NAIA they may not be as big or as fast, or as strong," he says of his players. "Or they may come out of successful high school programs where they may not gain the notoriety the other guys do. They may be later qualifiers—meaning that it takes them a little longer to get their test scores."

We acknowledge that St. Francis, their opponent, is sometimes a halfway house for these nonqualifiers. I ask Bell about his Division I experiences, and some of the differences he sees here, at the NAIA level.

"Division I ball is about selling that image. It's about big business. Their guys—they call them 'blue-chippers'—are just guys who are bigger, stronger, faster, and more physically proficient at an earlier age. That's why you see a lot of freshmen playing on that level. But there's a fine line there between fantasy and reality. The question exists between 'Do I really want a good education?' or 'Do I just want to play on television or try to go to the next level?' But I'm thankful that no matter where I've been or who I've worked with, the number-one goal has been to recruit guys that fit our program, like Cam Cameron, Howard Schnellenberger."

Like many coaches, Bell has distilled his recruiting distinctives into four main points: Be a champion on the field. Be a champion in the classroom. Be a champion in life. Be a champion for Jesus Christ.

"Recruiting is tough anywhere that you end up," he explains. "Why? Because if you're working with a seventeen- or eighteen-year-old, trying to show him the options he has . . . it's just like buying a house . . . you have to go in there and weigh all of the options out there. Are they comfortable with the surroundings, and the total package the university has to offer? But what is the major thing about recruiting? Assets. Money. Do you have the funding to travel and go recruit the kind of student that they want to have here? You have to travel and go throughout the United States. The last thing is facilities. What kind of facilities do you have? The kids look at that first—what does it look like?"

Taylor's facilities, at least for football, have changed very little since 1995. There have been minor upgrades to the field house, but by and large it's the same building now that it was ten years ago. The university recently built a multimillion dollar, state-of-the-art workout facility for general student use, which includes an indoor track, a lavish weight room, and several multipurpose courts. This is because prospective students in the ultra-competitive private school market deemed their previous workout facilities "unacceptable." All to provide a place for 135-pound philosophy majors to lift weights and jog on treadmills.

"You have to see things evolve and make sure you're keeping up with the times at your particular school," Bell continues. "We can't have the same scale as somebody else because we don't know their resources. University of Texas has unlimited resources . . . some schools don't. That's the reality of it."

I ask Bell about the tenuous link between religion and winning at a place like this. Whether it's more important to be a "good guy" or to win football games.

"My philosophy on coaching has always been that . . . [ministry] . . . that's my mission and it's something that I believe in. They need to understand the reality of life, and that life is not easy. I'm going to love them, but I'm going to show them what's right.

"When you are in a private Christian school, and teaching people about what's right—and I mean what God says—in this setting it's a lot easier because there's no fingers to point at you.

Whereas at public institutions they're more apt to question that, and challenge you on the issue."

Bell's predecessor, my college coach, was universally lauded as a "good guy," but like most Taylor football coaches, found it increasingly difficult to win football games in a competitive conference against schools without many of the same challenges. Of all of the coaches listed in Taylor's media guide, only a few, and most of those in decades previous, had winning records for their careers.

"It's a night and day difference from the previous guy," Bell continues. "The Lord has a passion for all his people and loves them . . . but in Second Timothy, it says 'I'm going to chastise you' and 'I'm going to teach you.' They need to understand the difference between reality and fantasy . . . and understand that they can't have their way all the time. But the Bible also says that you run the race to win, not to finish second. You have to teach them what's right, love them no matter what, but be intense. Jesus wouldn't have had to turn over the tables in the temple if people had been obedient. If you're not being obedient we need to get your attention. He said, 'You're not allowed to do this in my father's house.' "

He was fully good, but dangerous. Speaking of dangerous, I ask, how do you get your guys ready to face the best team in the nation, tomorrow?

"Same way I get them ready for No. 20, No. 6, and still have an opportunity to win. We're very young, playing a lot of freshmen and sophomores, but we're very competitive. Our responsibility is to go by God, play with a lot of heart, and go out and give your best. Your best has to be good enough.

"Saturday is our evaluation period," he says. "We compete. Am I giving my best effort?"

Bell was the first minority hired at Southwest Missouri State as a football coach. He also spent a couple of very rough years at

Jackson State University, a historically black institution. I also learn that he was the first coach in school history to integrate the program and that, combined with his losing record, couldn't have done much to ingratiate him to the powers that be. It has been my experience in football that if one is going to rock the boat, so to speak, one had better be extremely successful. Only eccentric winners are tolerated. Eccentric losers are eliminated (see: John L. Smith, Michigan State University).

I find the following, researching Bell online, a petition circulating through a Web site called "BellGottaGo.com" calling for his dismissal from Jackson State.

Web site: www.bellgottago.com
Description/History:
October 21, 2004

Thousands of JSU fans are fed up with second-year head football coach James Bell. Bell is NOT doing a good job and is not producing victorious results!

Petition:

To: Jackson State University Athletic Department and President Ronald Mason:

Because of our love and support of Jackson State Football, we the following students, faculty, alumni, and fans of Jackson State University, sincerely and urgently request that you fire James Bell as head football coach immediately.

Our request is based on Coach Bell's total ineptitude in dealing with all facets of JSU's Football program since the inception of his hiring and his total lack of experience as a head coach on the collegiate level.

WE THE UNDERSIGNED agree that since Coach Bell can't properly train our players, run imaginative, winning plays or develop a Championship Team, then it's time for him to go! Please sign and share your comments on this matter!

"Sincerely, The Undersigned"

I ask him about the Jackson State experience, in light of the fact that in my experience at least, sports has been one of the few present examples of racial harmony in our culture.

"I would agree with that," he says. "Jackson was my second head-coaching job. It was a different experience because it was a historically black college in the middle of Jackson, Mississippi. One of the issues there was still money and facilities. Those are the things you always have to overcome. When I got there, your heart has to be, 'How can I shepherd my flock? What can I do to make their time here better?'"

How was that philosophy embraced there?

"When you believe what you believe, and are vocal about it, you'll be persecuted," he says, cryptically. "The other big part of that is change. Any time change is on the horizon, that's going to be hard to face. That's something that I think was a big battle. It did exist. We did make changes there. It's a different place now. We redid the locker rooms . . . got the idea from Michigan State."

But redoing the locker room is one thing; changing the course of history for a school is yet another. He still hasn't mentioned the fact that he recruited white players to the school. I ask him if there was a difference in coaching an all-black team at JSU, as opposed to a mostly white TU squad.

"I didn't coach all black players because I went out and recruited white players," he says. "I went out and hired white coaches, too."

That must have been a shock to the University's system, I tell Coach Bell.

"I bring in talent, regardless of color," he says, bristling a bit. "I bring in the right people. I laugh at all the stuff I've been through, but if you interview my wife it's a different story."

I can imagine that it would be, and I also doubt that he laughs in private at what he's been through. Coaching is often the hardest on those who surround the coach—wife, children, and parents. Bell gives me an old media guide from Jackson State, and flipping through it I am stopped by the white faces—Steven Haren, a quarterback from Menlo Park, California, and Tommy Whitten, a WR from Brandon, Mississippi. Haren, the team's starting quarterback in 2005, struggled along with the rest of the squad, throwing 9 INTs as compared with only 5 TDs. Jackson State finished 2–9 in 2005, being outscored 365–201. Bell was removed as head coach in the middle of the season. Neither Haren or Whitten are currently enrolled at Jackson State, and I will try, unsuccessfully, to reach both of them.

"I'm a white guy at an HBCU," Haren said in an interview with *The Blue and White Flash*, a campus paper. "I have had to meet new people because it is about forming relationships on and off the field. The people take football down here as their passion; it's their way of life and you want to play in a big game atmosphere like this."

"Sometimes you're a trailblazer . . . a pioneer," Bell continues. "Sometimes you say 'Lord, don't send me down that creek' but you have to go down that creek to make it easier on the next person. What we did was make it better, and that was our responsibility."

Bell and I are on the move now, walking past Jim Wheeler Memorial Stadium, and into the Don Odle Gymnasium. Bell has some deliveries to make in the athletic offices, and wants to show me how they have upgraded the athletic facilities since I left. We walk through the gym foyer, past the pictures of teams gone by, the faces predominantly white.

When I was here, I tell Bell, Taylor never had more than a handful of black athletes on its football teams. And if the isolation I felt as a small-town kid with no money was any indicator, it must have only been intensified by their skin color.

"Well," he replies, "we've got thirteen now."

The morning of the game I wake up in my childhood room, pull back the curtain, and discover the type of day they generally try to portray in the admissions brochures—cool, clear, and sunny. Even the brutal Taylor wind has subsided.

At a few minutes before the 1 P.M. start, the stands at Jim Wheeler Memorial Stadium are still largely empty. It has been several years since I have been to a small-college football game, and the differences between this experience, and my experiences covering Big Ten and MAC football are many.

Covering those games, I am usually mailed a parking pass and credential by an unnamed drone in the Sports Information Department at said Big University—a department that could also be called "people who make it hard for you to get what you need." These are the folks responsible for media guides that are roughly as thick as New York City phone books, containing nuggets of critical information like "a history of equipment managers at (name omitted) university" or the fact that a full 85 percent of offensive linemen in the Midwest list "hunting and fishing" as their favorite off-season activities, followed closely by "weight lifting."

I typically affix my parking pass, usually marked with a distinction like "Lot 62 East," to the rearview mirror and set off on the business of working my way past drunk frat boys and tailgating alumni to find the elusive Lot 62 East. Once there, it's another long walk to the media entrance, and then a long ride up a crowded elevator with other media types who all seem older than me and who all seem to, somehow, know each other. Typically, I am issued a seat in a press box that is approximately sixty-eight stories above ground level and behind glass, giving one the feeling of watching a game sitting a long way away from a really small television.

Postgame I wind my way though the bustling press box for another long elevator ride down to the press conference, which usually takes place in a small classroom, filled with more media types who, again, all seem to know each other. One by one, the athletes are brought in, usually still wearing their football pants and undershirts, with sandals replacing their cleats. If the players are newly minted stars, they have a somewhat stunned, deer-in-the-headlights look about them—in awe of the whole situation. The seasoned stars sport bored expressions and have already become adept at the art of talking without saying anything—spinning out phrases like "the game really slowed down out there for me today" and "I have to give all the credit to my offensive line . . . and Jesus Christ."

Is this Christian rock?" my dad asks, as the rock beats play through a tinny sound system on the field. This, also, is new since I was here. In years past, warm-ups took place in relative silence in front of the empty stands.

"It must be," I reply, "because I've never heard it before."

As Taylor is a conservative Christian college, there is none of the rap and metal that fills a normal stadium on Saturday afternoon, and minus that, the proceedings take on a slightly more aristocratic flavor. The fans trickle in—girls I went to school with who used to wear jeans and sweatshirts now look like Talbots models, sporting pantsuits and pushing strollers. The picture of the successful mommy. Many of the guys wear scarves over sweaters with no jacket, a sartorial choice that you will find only on chilly fall afternoons at private schools like these.

In the South end zone we stand a little slack-jawed, in awe of the team that St. Francis has produced, which continues to pour out of their locker room in the adjacent Taylor gymnasium. They number nearly a hundred, and wear dark blue metallic pants, silver helmets, and white jerseys.

"That's just the travel team," my dad comments, as the thickly muscled Cougars work their way onto the field. The Cougars will outweigh their protestant counterparts by over twenty pounds on the offensive and defensive lines and look, by all accounts, to be the more athletic group. Many of them have tattoos.

Slowly, as the seconds tick away before game time, we are approached by a number of apprehensive Taylor fans who apologize, preemptively, at the game we're about to see. One couple, friends of my parents, approach us along the sidelines, adorned in leather jackets, purple and gold Taylor caps, and giant buttons that bear images of themselves in college. The requisite jokes are made along the lines of "who's the young guy on the button?" Ha-ha. Finally, the conversation gets a little morose. We are informed that six Taylor starters, including leading rusher Anthony Lee, have been suspended—not for drinking, drugs, or other such mayhem—but for participating in an "air band" or lip-synch competition that is a yearly tradition on campus. The University of Miami this is not.

"The coach was concerned they wouldn't have their minds on football," our friend says, gravely.

"Well, all we can do is pray for them," says the woman.

After a moment, my dad replies: "I don't think the Lord himself could beat St. Francis today."

The game unfolded like so many Taylor games in my past—fans arriving late (midway through the second quarter), and a feisty but hard-fighting team being quickly overwhelmed by its opponents.

St. Francis was as good as advertised, going 67 yards on its first drive, to gain a lead that it would never relinquish.

We are met in the stands by an older Taylor alum, who played offensive line for my father, who coached the position for one season, in 1982. His son, Trevor, is now a freshman WR for the Trojans. I ask him how Trevor, an Indiana high school all-star, is adjusting to college football.

"Like any wide receiver, he thinks every pass should be thrown to him," he replies. Unfortunately many of Taylor's passes do not even reach their intended targets, as their starting quarterback, out with injury, was replaced by a 185-pound sophomore who three weeks ago was a wide receiver.

Scoring at a breakneck pace, the Cougars stretch their lead to 35–0 before halftime. They have scored in a variety of creative ways—including a fake punt that was snapped directly to a full-back, who then raced untouched into the end zone.

After halftime we make our way around to the St. Francis sideline, weaving our way through the throng of alumni congregated around the stadium entrance. Many are chattering with their backs turned to the game, unaware that there is even a game happening, and that their school is enduring a colossal beat-down.

St. Francis has filled the small section of bleachers on its side of the field with enthusiastic fans. They have their backups in now, and their sideline has taken on a festive atmosphere, with starters lounging on the bench, chatting each other up after a job well done. The third quarter, though, is the strongest of the game for Taylor, who forces turnovers to stop both of the Cougars' offensive drives. And to their credit, Trojan linebackers Paul Passiales and Brandon Kightlinger never stop hitting—both pacing the Taylor defense in tackles.

Early in the fourth quarter, USF uses an 80-yard run to score, then closes out the scoring with a 2-yard plunge.

TU's deepest penetration is to the Cougars' six-yard line following an Andre Payne 40-yard carry with only twenty-three ticks remaining on the clock. However, a penalty moves them back five yards and the Trojans run out of time before they can find the end zone. The final score is 49–0.

Several weeks later I am back on campus to teach a class in the Communication Arts Building, and I pick up a copy of *The Echo*, the Taylor University student newspaper, which has run a review of my first book. I am stopped by a headline on the sports page which reads FRUSTRATION GROWS FOR TROJANS: OHIO-DOMINICAN SHUTS OUT TAYLOR 21–0. The article goes on to describe the loss, which puts Taylor at 0–6 in the Mid-States Football Association, and 1–7 overall.

To say that the Trojans had a rough outing offensively would be an understatement. They managed only 77 total yards and eight first downs the entire game against a team coached by Dale Carlson, who spent several years as Taylor's head coach in the early 1990s. The quotes in the article are telling.

"The quarterback needs to look downfield and find the open receiver," said senior WR Randy Dunbar. "Quarterback is the hardest position to play on the field. [The quarterbacks] have a tough job, but they could be doing better."

Ouch. That sound you hear, Randy, is the bus running over your teammate, who was thrown there by you. There's more.

"The play calling really needs handed over to the offensive co-ordinator," said senior WR Mike Simon. "He took it over for the final two games of last year, and we averaged 30 points. Maybe we could look towards him as a resource to better improve our offense."

On one hand they are just college kids venting their frustration at a losing season, but on the other hand, they are reflections of an athletic culture where restraint runs a distant second to self-expression. They are children of TO and Ocho Cinco.

And it's sad to see that even in utopia, wide receivers are still divas.

CHAPTER 2

THE GAME OF THE CENTURY:
CHARLIE "MAD DOG" THORNHILL AND MICHIGAN STATE VERSUS NOTRE DAME

THE SPARTAN STADIUM CLUB foyer possesses the requisite amount of glitz that one would come to expect from a Big Ten football program. A giant, gilded statue of "Sparty" provides the focal point for the room. I learn that this is the "old" Sparty, brought inside because its broad shoulders were decaying as a result of decades worth of Michigan winters and collegiate vandalism.

I am here for a reunion in honor of the 1966 Michigan State Spartans and their "Game of the Century" against Notre Dame forty years prior. The current Spartans, an as-yet undefeated squad led by NFL draft worthy Drew Stanton at quarterback, will face Notre Dame and its all-world Heisman lock Brady Quinn tomorrow evening.

My entry to this exclusive soiree was brokered by a few old friends in the MSU development office. I am whisked upstairs in a stainless steel elevator to the club suite, lovingly named in honor of the highest bidder—in this case LaSalle Bank Club. These suites are popping up in college stadiums across the country, which are beginning, more and more, to look like NFL stadiums. Their purposes are twofold—the entertainment of rich alumni and the wooing effect on seventeen-year-old recruits.

As such, it is an appropriately bedazzled room. Lots of brushed wood, green carpeting, and a television visible roughly every seven degrees of head rotation. I grab my nametag and immediately realize that I, along with the guys from ESPN Classic, will stand out from the crowd. It is truly only former players, their spouses, and a couple of glad-handing wealthy alumni types who fill the room.

Bubba Smith, famous first for his performances as a defensive lineman for the old Spartans and Baltimore Colts, and later for his performances as Hightower in the *Police Academy* movie series, is holding court in the center of the room, ensconced in a giant leather chair, signing autographs. Smith is wearing a uniform reserved only for the very famous—a velvet jogging suit.

I walk past row after row of gleaming green Spartan helmets, reproduced by a company called Helmet Hut, to meet the exact specifications worn by each player. The helmets are era-correct, right down to the antiquated facemasks and suspension-helmet webbing. Each player will receive, in addition to the helmet, a DVD of the '66 game as well as an authentic game program.

Notre Dame came into East Lansing in 1966 having not won a National Championship since 1953, which by their standards at the time was a long drought. They were, however, ranked No. 1. Host Michigan State, who had been upset by UCLA in the Rose Bowl the previous year, costing them a national title, entered the game ranked No. 2. This was the first time in twenty years that a college football contest was given the "Game of the Century" tag by the national media (though it would happen a few times since), and the not-new phenomena of Notre Dame "subway alumni" as well as an equal number of Notre Dame haters made this a must-see event.

Notre Dame halfback Rocky Bleier wrote in *Fighting Back*:

The train ride to State was another experience. Their fans were standing on the platforms in Battle Creek and Kalamazoo, some even stood along the tracks, in cornfields and on dairy farms—jeering and holding sheet signs: "Bubba for Pope," "Hail Mary, full of grace, Notre Dame's in second place." None of that, however, was as bad as our arrival in East Lansing. As I disembarked, I noticed the metal steps were slippery with ice. Behind me, I heard a yelp. It was my roommate on the road, Nick Eddy. He'd slipped, missed his grab for the handrail, and reinjured his bruised shoulder. He was doubled over, crying with pain and with the instant realization that he couldn't play in the biggest game of his career. People called it "The Game of the Century" that year . . . which was not especially important, because somebody makes that statement about one game in nearly every college football season. What is significant is that even today, some experts are still calling it "The Game of the Century."

In the pregame warm-up, I was entranced (almost dizzy, or high!) at the sight and sound of the 76,000+ fans in Spartan Stadium. Nothing I ever experienced on a football field, before or since, has equaled it. The chants rocked and swayed at a deafening level. Try to imagine quadraphonic speakers blasting the Rolling Stones at full volume. It was like that . . . clearly, the edge of insanity.

Oddly, the game was not shown live on national TV. Each team was allotted one national television appearance and two regional television appearances each season. Notre Dame appeared on national TV earlier against Purdue, and though ABC executives did not even want to show the game anywhere but the regional area, a letter-campaign from the West Coast and the South forced ABC to air the game on tape delay.

As has become part of "Game of the Century" lore, injuries played a large role in the outcome of the game. Notre Dame halfback Nick Eddy would famously hurt his shoulder stepping off a train in East Lansing. Irish quarterback Terry Hanratty was knocked out after absorbing a sack in the first quarter by Spartan defensive lineman Bubba Smith. Michigan State held a 10–0 lead early in the second quarter. But the Irish came back, and tied the game in the third quarter. Notre Dame had the ball on its own 30-yard line with 1:10 to go, and needed about 40 yards to attempt a game-winning field goal. But Coach Ara Parseghian chose to run the clock out, preserving the tie and Notre Dame's No. 1 ranking. Parseghian's end-of-the-game strategy was famously captured by *Sports Illustrated* icon Dan Jenkins as "Tying one for the Gipper." However, Notre Dame showed that it could stymie the defending national champs on the road, without the services of its own starting quarterback and star runner. And the quarterback who took the snaps for the Irish, Coley O'Brien, was diabetic and spent much of the afternoon exhausted to such an extent that he could no longer throw the football.

The game ended in a 10–10 tie.

Charlie "Mad Dog" Thornhill, the Spartan linebacker whom I was supposed to meet here, is nowhere to be found. So I wander the room, sticking to the walls. I speak with Dugald Tryon, the old team manager, and George Webster, the All-American linebacker who has lost both legs to diabetes.

Finally, I approach an old coach, a man I recognize to be Henry "Hank" Bullough, who was an assistant coach on the '66 team, a former coach of the Buffalo Bills during the unfortunate post–OJ Simpson era, and is now the "face" of MSU football alumni, namely because he shows up to everything. I have been told that he is a little, to put it charitably, prickly—which is another way to say that he likes being made to feel special. Bullough is short and thin—not typical dimensions of an offensive line coach—and stands by himself sipping a Coke. I think this might be the right time to ask him a couple of questions.

I extend a hand, a gesture that goes unreturned.

"Coach Bullough, I'm Ted Kluck and I'm writing a chapter in a college football book on the '66 team," I start. "I wondered if I could ask you a couple of questions about Charlie Thornhill?"

"Who let you in here?" he asks. Sometimes people are joking when they ask this type of question. Bullough, though, is definitely not joking.

Charlie "Mad Dog" Thornhill would like you to think that he doesn't enjoy being called "Mad Dog" anymore, whereas he actually enjoys it very much. He is of shorter stature than I would imagine from a former All-Big Ten linebacker, who has produced two sons who have also gone on to play with distinction at Michigan State University.

I am met at Thornhill's suburban home by, ironically, a mad dog—a little yipper who swirls around my lower leg with the same fury and authority that its owner brought to Spartan Stadium in the mid-sixties. Thornhill greets me with the requisite vise-grip football handshake, and is decked out, head to toe, in Spartan regalia.

If the 1966 tilt was the Game of the Century (so dubbed by those in the media), then the 2006 game will become equally famous for the monumental collapse suffered by the Michigan State Spartans. In recent Spartan fashion they found a way to snatch defeat from the jaws of victory, blowing a considerable lead in a fourth-quarter downpour in which it was raining real rain, in addition to Notre Dame touchdowns.

Michigan State, up 31–14 at halftime, looked ready to cruise to victory on the gigantic legs of running back Jehuu Caulcrick, a 260-pound banger in the mold of "The Nigerian Nightmare," Christian Okoye. Caulcrick, who was born in Liberia but moved on to collect three All-State honors in New York as a prep star, had a ridiculous 111 yards on eight carries, averaging a gaudy 13.9 yards per rush. But inexplicably, the coaches stopped calling his number. Stanton carried the ball nineteen times, and attempted twenty-two passes, one of the last of which was intercepted and taken to the house by Notre Dame's Terrail Lambert to seal a 40–37 victory for the Irish on Saturday night. Notre Dame coach Charlie Weis dedicated the win to Ara Parseghian.

For head coach John L. Smith, the game was a monumental failure on a number of levels. One, his club cavorted and gyrated in front of Touchdown Jesus last year, planting their flag in the middle of Notre Dame Stadium after a win last season, starting a flag-planting subplot that was important only to the Spartans. Two, the game was played on national television—on ABC's Saturday night game of the week lash-up, with Brent Musberger presiding. Musberger can make a second-quarter rush for no gain sound like a collision between two transatlantic oil tankers. He is a national treasure.

Thornhill, not surprisingly, is disgusted when I visit with him on the Monday evening following the game.

"It was kind of great to see all of the old guys back . . . Bubba Smith, Jimmy Raye, George Webster. It brought back old memories of our game," he says of being introduced on the field before kickoff. "I wanted to dress out in my uniform and go slam somebody. All of us did. We couldn't understand what was happening."

Thornhill's son, Caleb, is a starting linebacker on this year's squad. He led the team with 5 tackles on Saturday night, and was despondent postgame.

"I talked to my son outside the locker room after the game and he was very disappointed," says Thornhill. "He couldn't believe Notre Dame came back the way they did. I wish we could have beaten those guys, but it wasn't meant to be. I told him that things happen for a reason, and you have to rebound and get ready for the Big Ten opener."

So shocked were the Spartans that they sent a contingent of players out to guard midfield against a retaliatory flag-planting from the Irish, who apparently were too busy celebrating the victory with their fans to care much.

"He didn't point any fingers," Thornhill says of his son. "I do the fingerpointing. I don't want him doing that."

I was struck, watching the glitzily packaged ABC presentation of the game complete with a highly produced highlight intro backed by a rock band, by how much the game has changed since 1966.

"Speaking for myself . . . and I never felt this way before . . . I felt the same way I felt back in '66," he says. "The adrenaline. It felt different for me. I think it was all the hype, all of the stuff Weis said about never losing to MSU again. When I played I put ND on my helmet just to get them mad. It was a different feeling this time for me. But my doctor says I have to learn how to relax up in the stands. I might have to take up NASCAR racing."

For some reason, I don't see that happening. Thornhill continues to talk about the changes in the game.

"The blocking schemes are different," he says. "The linemen do more holding. And the lines are more spread out, which makes it easier to run. In my day it was three yards and a cloud of dust.

"I think with that '66 game you could see that the game itself had a major impact on college football. The coverage of college football and so forth. Nobody up to that time ever had seven hundred news reporters coming in from all over the world. A guy in Michigan tried to sell his grocery store in exchange for some tickets. The multitude of the game was so huge."

Why do you think that was?

"You had No. 1 and No. 2 playing each other," he says. "It was a national championship type game between the two of us, and you had Alabama trying to make some noise in there too, but nobody paid attention to them because of the segregation."

I ask Thornhill if Alabama's reluctance to integrate held them out of serious national title consideration.

"Absolutely. For the most part the news reporters knew this, which is why they stayed No. 3 in the country," he says. "I have kind of a soft spot for Alabama anyways, because Bear Bryant got me up here."

Bryant was a key figure in Thornhill's recruiting. Coming out of high school in Virginia, Thornhill was so highly regarded that some thought he might make a leap directly into the NFL with the Baltimore Colts. Bryant, who hadn't yet integrated the Alabama squad, nonetheless encouraged Thornhill to go north to Michigan State.

"It [recruiting] wasn't as big a deal as it was with my sons," he says. "I was just happy that somebody wanted me at their university. I was humbled. The University of Maryland, which didn't have any blacks, was looking at me . . . along with Tulane, Iowa, and all of the black schools. The thing about the black schools is that they wanted me but I would have had to pay for my books."

I ask Thornhill if being a "first" held any appeal.

"I wasn't willing to be a Jackie Robinson," he says. "I didn't have the right persona to endure the things he endured. I was kind of a feisty sort of person and I wasn't going to take any crap. I wasn't going to be a trailblazer.

"It was difficult enough to come up here to Michigan State and the culture shock there," he continues. "But if I'd had to go to one of those places the National Guard would have had to go to school with me every day."

Thornhill, recently, was voted the best schoolboy athlete ever to come out of the state of Virginia, from 1900 to the present.

"The guy from the Baltimore Colts came to my high school," he says. "I thought they wanted me to go from high school right to the Baltimore Colts."

Was it realistic? Was that an option you actually entertained?

"I entertained it in my mind," he says, "but in reality I had to say 'no way.' I didn't think I was ready."

We discuss his experiences reliving the recruiting process through his sons and how the athletes, now, drive the recruiting ship.

"I couldn't believe with Josh how these schools come after these kids, coming on the recruiting trail," he says. "I told him he would not wear No. 41, which was my number. I said that there was going to be enough pressure on him. Bottom line, I wish he had gone to UCLA or somewhere. Sometimes you have to spread your wings and fly.

"As far as the recruiting though, we were interested in what these schools had to offer on the academic side of things. We didn't care about the facilities or anything because all of these big programs have basically the same stuff."

Josh, his oldest son, was an honor student who aspires to one day become a physician's assistant.

"Ohio State did not put a lot of emphasis on the educational aspect of things," he says. "Northwestern and, to be fair, Michigan both emphasized it quite a bit. But when we went to Michigan I couldn't wait to get out of that place."

Why?

"I just didn't like the damn place," he says. "The place itself made me nervous. It was Ann Arbor, Michigan. When I first came up here I didn't know the rivalry between Michigan and Michigan State, but they gave me a full dose when I got here. And then playing against them made me more intense.

"The only time I enjoyed going to Ann Arbor was to whup their ass . . . I told Josh, and I left it up to him, I said if you pick

UM I will never sit in the damn stadium. I told him I'd watch from outside."

I have decided to ask Mad Dog Thornhill to show me the DVD of the game that he received the other night, at the reunion. He has said that he doesn't like watching himself on film, but something tells me he will enjoy this very much.

My first reaction is that Spartan Stadium looks almost exactly the same today as it did in 1966, save for the monstrous addition of new suites and club seating that is brand new this season. Both offenses often run double tight end formations, and full house backfields, meaning that there is usually only one wide receiver in the formation. The linebackers, at their farthest, play only three yards off the line of scrimmage.

Thornhill gets me situated on a sofa, but he will stand and pace for the entirety of the game. I ask him again about the differences in college football, then and now.

"We spent more time on the practice field than in the classroom," he says. "These kids today it's all classroom, classroom, meetings, meetings."

Knowing the answer already, I ask if he thinks the game was more physical when he played.

"Yes. Yes. Absolutely. These kids don't hit nearly as hard as we did. Practice was more intense than it is now. For me to sit up there and actually think you're seeing a great game . . . kids miss so many tackles. They're not teaching kids that anymore. The kids don't know how to wrap up with the shoulder pads and run through the guy. It's happening in professional ball too.

"We used to call my right forearm 'the Devil,' as in give 'em the Devil," he recalls, when I remark about the pad on his right forearm. On-screen, the offense is struggling.

"I didn't like my offense that year. Every time we gave them the ball inside the 40 I felt like they should score. It used to piss us off because they were treated better . . . the coaches would let them practice in a gymnasium when the weather was bad, but the defense was always out on the field. I hate to even look at this, offensively," he says, as the images flicker above.

"People talk about old school. Old school was rugged type of football. Ray Lewis plays like old school guys. But people pay money to see touchdowns scored."

There aren't many touchdowns scored in the Game of the Century, which flickers above us from Thornhill's entertainment center. Listening to Thornhill, I am expecting to see a bloodbath of perfect form tackling, fundamentals, and Old Time Football. It looks, to me, though, like a regular football game, with lots of punting and lots of three-and-outs. A Regis Cavender touchdown and a Jim Kenney field goal comprise all of the Spartan points. Irish kicker Joe Azzaro tied the game in the fourth quarter, and the game would remain, famously, a tie.

"If you take that game the other night," he says, "and let's say there was a big hit where somebody just laid somebody out. People would still be talking about it. But we did it every other play. I mean, I made sixteen tackles against Notre Dame, but that was just a normal thing. If I made twenty-two or twenty-three tackles, which I did before, that wouldn't be a big deal."

I ask Thornhill if it upsets him that the Michigan State football community has adopted this game, a 10–10 tie, as the greatest in its history. The game is legendary partly because Notre Dame, with the ball and a chance to win at the end, played for a tie.

"We were very unhappy campers in that locker room after the game," he recalls. "Like Duffy said, a tie is like kissing your sister."

Wrote Bleier in *Fighting Back*:

> Almost everybody was crying. The emotion of the game, the hitting and violent contact, was converted into the emotion of the locker room . . . the tears, the hugging, the trite phrases. Then Ara spoke

to us, "Men, I'm proud of you. God knows I've never been more proud of any group of young men in my life. Get one thing straight, though. We did not lose. We were Number One when we came, we fell behind, had some tough things happen, but you overcame them. No one could have wanted to win this one more than I. We didn't win, but, by God, we did not lose. They're crying about a tie, trying to detract from your efforts. They're trying to make it come out a win. Well, don't you believe it. Their season is over. They can't go anywhere. It's all over and we're still Number One."

Remarkably, eight Spartans from the '66 team were drafted the following year. Several, like Bubba Smith, Gene Washington, and George Webster, went on to distinguished pro careers.

"There were thirty-three NFL draft prospects in that game," Thornhill says. "Eleven guys from Michigan State made first-team All-Big Ten. Eleven. Something like fifteen All-Americans on the field.

"We were a very close unit, for the time," he says. "We didn't look at each other as black and white, we looked at each other as a family. During the training table, blacks have a tendency to eat together, and whites with whites. Duffy saw that one night and said, 'Dammit, I'm tired of blacks sitting on one side and whites sitting on another side!' So you better believe every time through the line I found me a white guy to sit with.

"I don't know too much about Michigan State and whether they do that today," he says. "But for us I could not believe how friendly people were up here. It's not like we really tried to get to know white people . . . white people wanted to get to know us!"

Thornhill was drafted in the ninth round by the New England Patriots, and didn't make it out of training camp.

"I didn't especially like pro ball," he says. "It was big business, just like any other job, and back then we got chicken-feed for salaries."

He spent several years playing in the Midwest Football League, with the Lansing All-Stars and Flint Sabres, and attempted a comeback in the Canadian Football League with the Hamilton Tiger-Cats.

Following his playing days, Thornhill spent twenty-one years with General Motors in Lansing, including time as a patrolman. In 1992, he became a sergeant-at-arms in the Michigan Senate. I ask him if the transition out of football and into real life was a difficult one for him.

"Life goes on," he says. "It's tough for a while. You try to find and take on other challenges . . . "

Unless people constantly ask you, around town, about the Notre Dame game.

"You gotta remember," he says, "this was the Game of the Century, where a lot of things occurred. This was big, I mean, this was huge."

I am celebrating Christmas in Nashville, Tennessee, when I receive news from a mutual friend that Charlie Thornhill passed away the day before. According to our friend, Thornhill, sixty-two, left his post as sergeant-at-arms in the Michigan Senate early, complaining of not feeling well. He died of heart failure on Thursday, December 21 at Ingham Regional Medical Center.

I last saw Charlie Thornhill in the concourse of Spartan Stadium earlier in the fall, after the Spartans had just lost to Big Ten doormat Illinois on homecoming. He was standing alone—rare for him, as he is gregarious by nature and something of a local celebrity—and waiting for his son Josh, who was honored on the field earlier in the day. I knew he would be upset by the loss, so I debated as to whether I should say anything to him at all. But I walked up to him and shook his hand. Not surprisingly, he greeted me with a warm smile and a kind word.

CHAPTER 3

THE FORTUNE TELLER:
PHIL STEELE

TO SAY THAT Phil Steele's offices, home of Northcoast Sports, leave a little to be desired in the way of outward adornment would be a vast understatement of things. On the outskirts of Cleveland, in Westlake, I exit I-90 onto Columbia Road, make a right past a McDonald's, and follow another road past row after row of low-slung industrial-parkish buildings that are no doubt home to lots of print shops and direct-mail companies. This is a place where "corporate culture" means a few minutes to smoke a cigarette on the loading dock. And this is a time of year—late February—in which Northern Ohio is covered with an oily, disgusting layer of decaying snow. Not exactly a prime location for America's foremost oracle of college football information.

I have decided to visit Steele because it strikes me that there may not be a human being on earth who has logged more hours watching football on television. Steele is famous (relatively speaking, of course) for his *College Football Preview* magazine, which weighs in at 288 pages, each page a graphic-designer's nightmare, filled from corner to corner with tiny text. Steele, it says in the magazine, writes every word himself, in addition to handicapping games and acting as something of an investment advisor for gamblers. The magazine, if one can get past the design challenges, is a veritable goldmine of information—archived stats, point-spreads, and five-deep depth charts for every team in Division 1-A.

After parking, I walk past an envelope place, and a loading dock that says DELIVERIES FOR UNITS A, B, AND C HERE. On the final door is a photocopied sheet of paper that says NORTHCOAST PUBLISHING. Inside, there is a cavelike room with probably fifteen employees at cubicles. The inside is as unadorned as the outside, save for a couple of giant pictures of NFL helmets on the walls. The employees at cubicles don't look up when I come in. They are busily working, doing whatever it is that they do. Many of them are surrounded by college team media guides—the glossy, catalog-like documents that college programs produce each year to promote and hype their clubs. I am early.

Joey Lucci, a young guy who works at the office, meets me at the door. "Phil likes to prepare," he says. "If I brought you in there fifteen minutes early he'd probably kill me. Let's grab lunch."

At lunch I learn Lucci's history with the company (five years), his favorite video game (Tecmo Super Bowl, using the Bears), his research specialty (the Big XII conference—"I could tell you anything about any of the teams") and his favorite cinematic genre (horror; he likes what Rob Zombie has done). To say that he is outgoing and gregarious by nature would also be an understatement. He grew up a Cleveland Browns fan and, like many Ohio kids, dreamed of wearing the Scarlet and Gray. Instead, he had a short tenure as a quarterback at NAIA Findlay University, and finally landed here, where he "reads about football all day."

Back inside the office, I am led into Phil Steele's office, which is appropriate for what I am envisioning as a football monk of sorts. It is filled, floor to ceiling, with paper—media guides, old magazines, notebooks, etc.—in an intricate catalog system decipherable by only Steele himself. One wall is completely devoted to televisions—twelve in all, each with VCR/DVR units built-in. And there are helmets—mini and full sized—all over the room. Steele, forty-seven, enters a few moments later and greets me warmly, taking a seat behind a large computer screen at command central. He looks not unlike Ron Jaworski, the old Eagles quarterback.

"I get in here at about 7 A.M. on Saturday mornings and stay until about midnight," he says. "I used to watch the Hawaii game until three in the morning but now that I have a baby at home I don't do that anymore. Sunday is pretty much the same, and now there are college games on almost every night of the week."

It strikes me that Steele has spent much of his adult life in this room. At my feet sit several cases of Diet Mountain Dew, perhaps the fuel that stokes the Steele engine.

"I've always loved football, and I've always been a numbers guy," he says. "When I was a kid, my favorite time of year was late summer, when my dad would take me down to the drugstore and tell me I was allowed to buy four college football preview magazines. I would start reading them in the car on the way home, and then take those magazines into my room and just disappear for weeks. If you had given me a thousand dollars and said, 'Buy whatever you want,' I would have bought those four preview magazines."

Though he didn't play high school or college football, Steele grew up in Cleveland cheering for the Browns, and now runs

Northcoast—part publishing company, part handicapping business—out of this nondescript Cleveland loading dock. I am led
through the back catacombs of the building, past two press oper-
ators and whirring machines, to a room piled high with stacks of
back issues that reach taller than my head. The back issues represent Steele's body of work.

After high school (Cleveland Public), Steele spent nine months
at a community college, before dropping out to manage a pizza
parlor. It was there, he says, that he learned the real ins-and-outs
of small business ownership. He was also looking for a way to
make football his full-time career.

"I used to see these ads in the sports pages for guys—they were
lying—who promised 70 percent accuracy and other crazy claims,"
he says. "I thought to myself, 'I can handicap football games,' so I
set up an 800-line in the back of my mom's house."

The 800-line soon became a small print shop, as Steele began
self-publishing football handicapping newsletters and maxing out
his personal credit cards.

"I spent $12,000 and only made $1,800 my first year," he says.
"I slept on a cot in the print shop for seven years. I never went
out to dinner."

Steele's parents even took out a second mortgage on their
house to fund their son's dream; after several years in the red,
however, even they lost patience.

"After five years, my dad sat me down and said, 'It's been fun
but it's time to get a real job,' " he recalls. Steele's father passed
away shortly thereafter, but Steele believes he was "pulling
strings" for him in 1989, his greatest season as a handicapper.

"I went 52–22 in 1989," he says. "That was legitimacy."

It would be fair to say that Phil Steele has "no life," but just as fair
to say that he has the life he wants, and the life many football
fans think they want.

"I have no idea how to work my cell phone, and if you take me to a dinner party I won't remember anyone's name," he says. "I know about football."

Steele is in at 7:30 in the morning on a normal day, and spends a great deal of time—when not watching live or taped football—speaking large amounts of text for his magazines into a Dictaphone, which is then transcribed by an assistant. After some digging in the office, Steele produces mock-ups for the team pages, each jam-packed with information on players, coaches, and lines. Northcoast Sports, having turned the corner in 1989, has grown gradually into the $4 million to $5 million operation it is today.

"I'm a workaholic," he says, unapologetically. His computer is papered with pictures of his new daughter. I ask him how this arrangement goes over with Mrs. Steele.

"We were just married four years ago and she knew the situation," he says. Steele has been known to miss weddings to watch preseason football. And when ESPN ushered in live college football virtually every night of the week, his life got even more complicated.

"I watch *Monday Night Football*, of course, and then usually Tuesday is a down night, when ESPN isn't running a game," he says. "But Thursdays and Fridays are usually game nights now too."

I ask him what, to me, seems like an obvious question: Do you ever get sick of football?

"I really don't," he says. "I get upset when my picks lose. I take that personally because it's my reputation on the line." Smiling, he looks at the door to the office. "I've put a couple of holes in that door over the years. Those weeks, the bad weeks, are the only times I get discouraged, and it's only because I put so much into it."

Steele produces handwritten notebooks with school conference names and years written on the front. He opens the notebooks to reveal meticulously detailed pages, on which lies information dating back to the 1980s. His handwriting is tiny.

These are the documents that would lay the foundation for what is now the *Phil Steele College Football Preview*. I ask Steele, if at any time during the lean years, he considered folding the tent and taking a "regular" job.

"You know, I was so busy that I really didn't have a whole lot of time to sit and consult with myself.

"We're trying to steer away from the gambling stuff," Steele says, as he thumbs through a copy of the magazine on his desk. "If you look through here, there's really no gambling stuff to speak of. The major critique is that there's too much writing on each page, but this is not for the casual fan. Most people pick up preview magazines for the glossy photos, but we're not about pictures as much as we're about information."

An article by Arne K. Lang in Steele's 2006 magazine claims that "an independent survey, uncorrupted by the obligations of advertisers, subsequently proved what the patrons of Gamblers Book Club already knew. For several years running, Phil's publication has been rated the most complete magazine of its kind."

According to the piece, the ratings were based on "a host of different variables blended into a complex mathematical formula that eliminates subjective opinions." These variables include "forecasting accuracy, information quality, information quantity, recapping information, and price."

"As far as the handicapping business, we're very unique in that we don't take people's numbers and we don't call them at home," Steele says. "Essentially we don't do the boiler-room sales stuff that is so common in this business." Steele says in his magazine that "football is what I do for a living, seven days a week, 365 days a year. If you are going to invest serious money in the stock market and had a job that was not in the market, odds are you would have an analyst who did nothing but study stocks for a living. As you can tell by the sheer volume of information, I write each of the 119 team previews myself, which basically puts me on the magazine 'deadline' from the end of December through the middle of May."

Steele preaches that gamblers should never exceed 5 percent of their bankroll on any one bet, and emphasizes that there is no such thing as a "sure thing." "If you don't gamble," he says in his magazine, "then I don't want to talk you into it." In the same piece, he goes on to decry the idea of a fixed game, saying, "Just the thought that a game could be fixed disgusts me. I am a football fan, and love the sport, and everything about it. I personally hope that no games are ever fixed, as it would taint the sport of football."

Indeed the magazine is bereft of almost all gambling content, save for a bikini-clad model here or there, espousing the virtues of Northcoast Sports. The model was nowhere to be found in the Northcoast offices.

"Most of those ads will be gone this year," he says. "I want to protect and treasure the game, and moving forward I want our publications to be purely about the game."

Though he puts out an NFL preview magazine that he says is "probably sixth-best" on the market, the college game, with its rivalries, is his real passion.

"I grew up during the Bo Schembechler/Woody Hayes era, which was kind of a golden era in college football," he says. "I love that the fans are more passionate at the college level. The NFL has gotten too corporate. The kids, the bands, and the fact that teams can really change from year to year with coaching and recruiting.

"I knew I needed to do a college football magazine in 1989 when a player named Moe Elewonibi, from BYU, received the Outland Trophy, which goes to the nation's top interior lineman," he says. "I bought four college preview magazines that year and none of them even mentioned Elewonibi as a starter. The thing is, most of those magazines are just slapped together using local newspaper writers, who don't necessarily have the time to investigate all of the rosters and statistics they're printing. We'll even find, at times, that the NCAA's stats are wrong. We've stopped telling the teams though, because they don't like hearing it."

Elewonibi went on to play several years in the NFL and CFL, and as of 2005 was still playing. Steele remembers him often as the inspiration for his long days now. They have never met and, as a handicapper, Steele has the odd distinction of knowing more about college football than almost anyone, but rarely, if ever, being able to interact with its players or coaches for fear of compromising the integrity of the game.

Steele's first college preview magazine had write-ups on eighty-eight teams, and beginning in 1998 the lineup included all Division IA schools. Currently, the magazine features a full two pages on all 119 teams.

While the gambling world is known for its acronyms, such as ATS, against the spread, Steele's magazine took the acronym concept to a whole new level, in order to squeeze these copious amounts of information into such a small space. The font can be described as "squint-print," and Steele uses VHT to indicate "Very Highly Touted" recruits, assigning a number that corresponds to the amount of "highly toutedness" ascribed to that particular player. It's a dizzying amount of information that walks the fine line between annoying and sublime. All of this, it seems, to help determine the performance of eighteen- to twenty-one-year-olds.

Steele gives himself deadlines each day during the production of the magazine—he needs to write for three hours, finish three teams, that sort of thing. His favorite part, perhaps, is the projection of "surprise teams" and "Heisman Trophy winners," which he picked correctly three years in a row in the late nineties.

"I was on Ohio State before their National Championship in 2002," he says. "I don't think any other writer even had them picked to win the Big Ten. I look beyond things like returning skill players to determine my rankings and picks. I look at close games from the year before—which games could have been different due to things like missed extra points or fumbles."

He adds that he picked Ricky Williams and Ron Dayne correctly as well, but that there is one projection on which he failed miserably.

"Timmy Chang. I picked him to win the Heisman Trophy, which, looking back is pretty embarrassing. That's the one I'd like to have back."

Steele has very little to say about the NFL Draft, except that it's become "too talk showish." And to add that once the players are out of his magazine—seniors are removed after their last game—they kind of cease to exist for him, as the production cycle begins anew with freshmen and transfers. When he is asked about corruption in college football, he simply says, "I put blinders on—I don't want to believe it." For Steele, I think, college football as he knows it is a manageable set of statistics each year—heights, weights, rankings, forty times, etc. To dabble in theories about corrupt boosters, or whether players should be paid is someone else's business. As for what he would change about the game, he says, "I like it the way it is."

As I begin to pack up and let Steele get back to his deadlines, talk turns back to family. I learn that Steele's mother is on the payroll and works somewhere in the facility.

"I really can't say enough about my parents and their sacrifice for me," he says, referencing the second mortgage that got him started. "My dad was a Marine Sergeant and he instilled a work ethic in me as a kid. If I asked for something he would say 'go out and shovel snow.' " Steele recounts a story from the beginning of his career, when he was tempted to just make up flyers touting made-up records on his plays. His father sat him down and reminded him that that was not the way he was raised.

"I remember a day in 1964 when I was only four years old," he says. "I was aware of sports back then but I didn't have a good concept of time. My mom took me to see a movie, *Dr. Doolittle*, and when I came back home my dad was in the kitchen smiling. I asked him why he was so happy, and he said, 'The Browns are winning.' I wanted to be like my dad, and I wanted to be with my dad, who was a huge football fan. I learned pretty early on that if I wanted to be with him, I would need to be watching football."

CHAPTER 4

THE TURNAROUND:
BRIAN LEONARD, GREG SCHIANO, AND THE RUTGERS FOOTBALL RENAISSANCE

COLLEGE FOOTBALL coaches are liars.

Just hours after assuring the media and Miami Dolphins brass of his desire to remain a Dolphin, head coach Nick Saban fled South Florida for tens of millions in guaranteed dollars, and the opportunity to become the latest in a long line of Alabama coaches who will probably fail to be Paul "Bear" Bryant. This is the same Saban who is famous for leaving Michigan State, leaving LSU, and now leaving the Miami Dolphins. Your classic coaching mercenary.

So when coaches preach to athletes about commitment, personal integrity, and trust, it rings a little hollow. Opportunism is the new commitment. And it's not just Saban (see Butch Davis, Tommy

Tuberville, Brian Kelly, Dennis Erickson), as late autumn has become the season for disappointed players and disillusioned fans.

Which makes what has happened at the State University of New Jersey at Rutgers all the more intriguing.

Brian Leonard's parents knew very little of Rutgers before Brian's older brother Nate went there to play linebacker. Nate, as his parents are quick to tell me, endured five knee surgeries, most memorably blowing out his knee on the terrible artificial turf at Three Rivers Stadium in Pittsburgh. Brian followed his brother there, committing to coach Greg Schiano as part of his first recruiting class, in spite of the fact that Rutgers was not known for football, unless one were to count sucking at football.

In fact, it was Brian, then a freshman, who replaced Nate in the Gouverneur (New York) High lineup after Nate first tore his ACL. Brian would rush for 100 yards in relief duty that day, and says that the fact that Rutgers stuck to its commitment to Nate— who attracted interest from Wake Forest, Syracuse, and Boston College—is one reason Brian signed with the Scarlet Knights.

"What was it like for us?" asks Mark. "Well, the faith was that his brother Nathan was already at Rutgers. Brian had made up his mind early. We took trips to Notre Dame and Syracuse, but his heart was at Rutgers."

Brian scored a state-record 696 points and amassed 5,854 yards as a high schooler.

"He believed in Coach Schiano," Laurie adds. "I remember after his first visit, I don't know if Coach Schiano hypnotized him or what, but he came out of there and said, 'People are going to think I'm crazy, but I'm going to Rutgers.' "

His parents are delightful. They are decked out, head to toe, in Rutgers football apparel, and occupy a spot in the East stands for Brian's last Senior Bowl practice. They are unassuming, especially when compared with other entourages that have begun to form as the All-Star game approaches. One Midwestern quarter-back must have brought fifty people with him—all decked out in team swag and virtually taking over the hotel lobby.

"This is the last time we'll be able to wear our Rutgers gear," says Laurie, from behind a pair of sunglasses. She and her husband are here to support Brian, and I can immediately tell that they are the right kind of sports parents. Nothing about them says "notice me, because my son will be a millionaire in a few weeks."

"We don't think about the money at all," says Mark, a manager at Time Warner Cable. "We're just so glad he didn't leave Rutgers early last year. He loves Rutgers and he wanted to come back and play for Rutgers. We're going to miss the college environment."

"Brian became the poster child for college football in Northern New York," says a family friend, somewhat dramatically, though I don't disagree with him. Leonard's mug was plastered on billboards along nearly every New Jersey highway, and his Heisman Trophy campaign saw him on the cover of the Rutgers Media Guide as well as the subject of his own Heisman Web site.

Leonard generated a good bit of buzz via one of his more bizarre athletic accomplishments—the Leonard Leap. Leonard has been known to leap up and grab a basketball rim, backwards, at a height of ten feet, six inches, and put that skill to work early in 2006. In each of his first three games he leaped over defenders during runs, his most memorable against Buffalo in which he leapt a defender standing almost straight up. The photographs of these leaps only added to Leonard's lore. He would follow that by posting twenty-five repetitions at 225 at the NFL scouting combine, tops among running backs, and running in the 4.4's—unheard of for a fullback and more than respectable for a tailback.

"It's good to get the Rutgers name out there," said Leonard in an interview for Scarletknights.com. "I didn't really like all the attention on me with the Heisman campaign, but anything to help Rutgers Football get its name out is great for the program."

"We never doubted Coach Schiano and his loyalty," adds Laurie. The word loyalty is mentioned several times. "He also brought academic integrity to the program. His academic advisors are amazing."

I express how pleased I am to see a school known for academics excelling, it seems in the right way, on the football field.

Leonard, this season, became Rutgers' all-time reception leader (207), and also holds the career record for touchdowns scored with 45. He is second all-time in all-purpose yards with 4,643, and fifth all-time at Rutgers in rushing. Perhaps most impressive, he did all of this from the fullback position—a position widely believed to be dead or at least heavily phased-out of most offensive schemes.

"He can play tailback though," says dad, watching this practice as though he is watching his son play for the first time. "See, they've got him lined up at tailback now."

Brian takes a handoff on the field and bounces through the defensive secondary, before heading to the sideline where he chats up Penn State All-American Paul Posluszny.

"He and Paul became fast friends working out down in Arizona, because they share the same agent [Mike McCartney]," Mark adds, thrilled that his son has made a high-profile friend. Posluszny was given the label of "best linebacker to play at Penn State" by none other than Jack Ham, himself an NFL Hall of Fame Penn State alumnus. He also collected the Butkus (nation's top linebacker in 2005) and Bednarik (nation's top defensive player in 2005 and 2006) awards during his tenure in Happy Valley.

Laurie, however, is more concerned about another player, Pittsburgh's embattled QB Tyler Palko, who has struggled in practice this week. "Some of these draft writers write some pretty unflattering stuff," she says, sympathetically, as Palko's mother walks down the stairs in front of where we are seated.

Getting a quality interview anywhere is tough, but I think it's a little tougher here at the Senior Bowl, where a security guard who looks just like Sammy Davis Jr. patrols the Mobile Convention Center lobby with a vengeance. It is after waiting here for some time that I give up on an interview with Leonard, and make the long walk back to the hotel, through a throng of fans who will wait in line for long hours on their feet to get the signature of their favorite college star. There are lots of grown men in college players' jerseys, which is always a little unsettling. Do they aspire to be just like their favorite nineteen-year-old when they grow up?

On the off-chance that it will work (it never does), I call the front desk and ask to be put through to Brian Leonard's room. They patch me through and Brian picks up on the second ring. His voice is higher than I expected, which has the same disarming effect as it has with other high-voiced athletes in violent sports. Usually football players try to channel James Earl Jones when speaking.

Within minutes I am in the room that Brian is sharing for the week with Posluszny, Penn State's All-World linebacker. The room seems positively engulfed by the two large men and their accumulated swag—game jerseys, practice jerseys, Under Armour gear, and a giant tub of protein powder. There is an Animal Planet program on the television, which is in keeping with Brian's father's admission that his son "can't watch more than half of a football game in one sitting. He loves the animal shows—if he wasn't a football player he'd probably be a vet."

Leonard is that rare football animal in that he is a white running back—a position inhabited almost exclusively, for whatever reason, by black players. However, he has gained the respect of his opponents, including Pitt linebacker H. B. Blades who said of Leonard: "He's a very, very underrated player . . . he's the best running back I've played against since I've been in college [Including Kevin Jones, Julius Jones, Walter Reyes, and Darius Walker].

That combination of power and speed is amazing. Some of the runs he makes in the open field, he can cut like a tailback. He jumps over safeties when they try and cut him, but then he runs over linebackers and defensive linemen. His combination of power and speed just makes him the best at what he does."

"It's just one barrier that you have to overcome as an athlete," Leonard says of the white running back stigma. "But we all have barriers and we all have to prove ourselves. Regardless of the fact that the NFL is dominated by . . . I don't know how you would says it, I don't know the right term . . . 'African-American' players at my position. You don't see many white guys back there. I still have to prove myself."

White running backs in the NFL have been scarce to say the least, with the most promising, including Mike Alstott and Rob Konrad, being shifted to fullback immediately upon entry into the pros. One has to go back to the Tommy Vardell (an unsuccessful pro) and Merrill Hoge eras to find much in the way of white runners.

Leonard is a little smaller than expected, having slimmed down from 238 pounds to 224 to prove that he can play tailback at the next level. He did it, he says, to show scouts his versatility at the next level. Leonard keeps constant eye contact, and is extremely polite. His only piece of jewelry is a small necklace bearing his number, 23; it's the kind of necklace you wear when you're in high school.

Leonard, along with head coach Greg Schiano, keyed what could be called a football renaissance at Rutgers. Schiano was named Coach of the Year after the team was nationally ranked since week three, tied a school record for victories, and won its first-ever bowl game.

In truly cinematic fashion, Rutgers registered its biggest win of the season, and kept its unbeaten streak alive, by shocking No. 3 Louisville 28–25 before a record crowd of 44,111 at Rutgers stadium. It was their first win over a ranked opponent since 1988.

Rutgers overcame an 18-point deficit and plodded into field goal range late in the fourth quarter, utilizing runs by Ray Rice of 20, 4, and 2 yards, as well as a key reception by Leonard.

Junior placekicker Jeremy Ito lined up to attempt a 33-yard field goal with seventeen seconds remaining, and pulled it to the left, however, Louisville jumped offsides, giving Ito (quite obviously but still charmingly nicknamed "The Judge") the opportunity to kick himself into Rutgers lore by converting 28 yards with thirteen ticks left on the clock.

"I told our kids at halftime [trailing 25–14] that we were playing well, we just had to get some plays and mix it up," said Rutgers head coach Greg Schiano in another interview. "Our guys did a great job of adjusting in the second half. It takes smart and committed kids to make those changes."

The win was the largest come-from-behind victory since October 9, 2004, when the Scarlet Knights overcame a 24-point differential at Vanderbilt. More importantly, it added a nationally televised flourish to what would become a historic season at Rutgers. It, in essence, closed things out the right way, and gave Schiano the firepower he would need to land another top-flight recruiting class.

In the sixteen-year history of the Big East Conference, Rutgers is only the fifth team to win eleven or more games in a single season, joining West Virginia, Louisville, Miami (Florida), and Virginia Tech. Heady stuff for a team that used to have trouble hanging with Temple.

"We changed that place around," Leonard says. "The fifth-year seniors took a chance to go there when it wasn't a good time to go there. We believed in coach Schiano's word from the beginning. We got guys that believed in the program and believed they could turn it around."

I ask Leonard what made Schiano, in this atmosphere of football mercenaries, somebody worth trusting. Leonard turned down offers from Syracuse and Notre Dame to hitch his wagon to a program that, at that time, was dismal. Schiano's predecessor, Terry Shea, went 11–44.

"You've got to trust your coaches," he says, "and a lot of people don't trust their coaches. If you trust your coach you respect him and you do what he tells you. He promised us by the end of our careers we'd go to bowl games. He gave his word and said, 'I'm gonna be here the whole time you're here.' Really a lot of coaches don't care about that.

"When he's on the field he's a coach—he's in your face, he's loud, and he'll correct you. But off the field if he realizes he's said something he shouldn't have said, he'll come off the field and apologize. You're not a friend on the field, but off the field he's a friend and a mentor.

I ask Leonard if he still gets nervous before games, specifically practices here at the Senior Bowl against the best competition the nation has to offer.

"I did as a freshman—the competition was so much better and it was such a new experience," he says. "But I feel like the only time you should be nervous on the field is if you're not prepared."

The scrutiny here, at the Senior Bowl, is intense, and Leonard is aware that every move he makes on the practice field is heavily analyzed.

"You drop a pass and it's on the Internet immediately," he says. "I don't read that stuff, but my agent tells me about it. It's crazy."

Leonard pauses to read through a litany of questions provided by NFL teams to potential draftees—have you ever been arrested? Is there any reason why our club shouldn't draft you? It is a questionnaire given to him by his agent to prepare him for the impromptu lobby interviews that happen during Senior Bowl week.

Leonard says that getting recruited by agents is "worse than getting recruited by colleges." He changed his telephone number midway through his Junior season. Many thought Leonard would turn pro after that season, but the player who said, "I've never had any money" turned down a potentially huge NFL contract, only to have his worst season, statistically, as a college player. He rushed for only 423 yards and 5 touchdowns and often played second fiddle to another sensational back named Ray Rice.

"Was it tough not getting the ball? It was, but I embraced the role, and I feel like this year was my most satisfying year," he says. "I talked to a lot of people after my junior year—scouts, agents, and Marco Battaglia who went to Rutgers and played several years in the league. Everybody told me 'go with your heart,' my heart was at Rutgers."

Before wrapping up we drift back to the dog-eared questionnaire on the table. The most important question, Leonard says, is the one where they ask how important football is in your life. "What do you say to that question?" I ask him.

"You gotta tell them the truth," he says. "You gotta tell them how much football means to you. Is football your life? What would you do without football?"

What would you do without football?

"I don't know. I just love football," he says. "I've loved it all my life. I don't know what I'd do without it. Just one-on-one competition along with the team competition. It's the best team sport in the world."

I hope he never has to find out what life is like without it. I ask him, finally, what he will miss most about Rutgers.

"Oh, man," he says, pausing. "I'm going to miss everything about that place."

It wasn't long ago that you would have been hard pressed to find ten New Jersey residents willing to spend an hour in a room with the Rutgers football coach. Today, we are winding our way through the New Jersey highway system, in search of the Birchwood Manor Country Club in Whippany, New Jersey. Eventually the nail salons and strip malls give way to large homes, acres of woodland, and actual living things.

"I think I just saw a rabbit," says my friend Cory, a native of Passaic, New Jersey, where true nature is scarce.

Inside the gilded Birchwood Manor around 1,000 men in chinos, business-casual, blue-collars, and everything in-between have gathered to hear their newly minted favorite football coach, Greg Schiano, fresh off several national Coach of the Year honors. Schiano is seated at the front of the room, underneath a chandelier that looks big enough to have been recovered from the Titanic. Right in front of him, on a raised stage, there are several moppy-haired adolescents playing U2 songs to warm up the crowd, who paid twenty dollars a head to be here.

I learn from an associate of Schiano's that he was summoned by the governor of New Jersey to attend the NCAA Women's Basketball Final Four to discuss a stadium deal, and that he has been inundated with speaking requests like these. He is also still attempting to coach his own football team through spring practice, which started a few days ago. Crazy to think that a guy who was probably teaching high school social studies and coaching a few years ago has ascended to these heights.

The event's emcee, a pastor from Jacksonville Chapel—which sponsored the event—introduces a long list of dignitaries in the room, including, no doubt, several heads of corporations who paid top dollar to be introduced as dignitaries, and New Jersey Senator Anthony Bucco. These are men who look like they've spent much of their lives in country clubs.

"With our built-in inferiority complex we were bracing ourselves all off-season to lose Schiano," says Cory. "But the state government mobilized and tried to find creative ways to keep him."

Schiano's off-season was front-page news almost daily, as he was courted by bigger programs, most notably the University of Miami, where he had previously served as defensive coordinator. Finally, in a stroke of integrity that is almost shocking, Schiano decided to honor his contract and stay in New Jersey.

Not being from New Jersey myself, I spend a little bit of time at the breakfast trying to get a feel for Rutgers' reputation around the state, so as to get a feel for what may have compelled Schiano to stay.

"It's the largest state university in New Jersey," says one guy, after stopping to think about it for a moment. "Lots of kids have an opportunity to go there," says someone else. What is obvious, though, is the proclivity of Rutgers swag visible almost everywhere throughout the state. Finally, the state of New Jersey has something to not only not feel inferior about, but to also be proud of.

Schiano is the first coach in school history to lead the football team to consecutive bowl appearances, and he had no less than fourteen players on the All-Big East team this season. Where other coaches have failed, he has succeeded in keeping key New York/New Jersey talent close to home, as evidenced by players like Brian Leonard.

Schiano is a young-looking forty-one years old, and opens the talk with the usual banquet joke, about "not beating anyone" his first few years at Rutgers, where he started 3–20. Schiano has a gap between his front teeth and looks a little bit like a beefier, more Italian David Letterman. Clearly, he is comfortable speaking in public, as this is something the modern-day coach-turned-CEO must do often.

"I was a linebacker at Bucknell and captain of the football team," he says. "After graduation I went up to Canada to play in the CFL and after six weeks they told me I wasn't good enough and sent me home.

"I didn't want to see anybody or be seen by anybody. I was ashamed and I wanted to hide."

Schiano then coached for a year at his former high school, and decided if he was to pursue a career in coaching, that he would need to take a graduate assistantship. He was hired as a graduate assistant at Rutgers.

"And then we all promptly got fired," he says. "I didn't like that too well."

Schiano then became a secondary coach at Penn State, where he had his first brush with the religion that would shape his life and decision-making.

"I was walking past the player's lounge after practice one day and I heard the team chaplain leading some of my defensive backs in a Bible study," he says. "My first thought was 'get away from my guys—you're going to make them soft!'

"Not long after that I was in the car with the same guy. I think we were on our way to a Fuddruckers somewhere in the Midwest to meet a recruit. That's the glitz and glamour of college coaching. Anyway, as we were riding along, he asks me, 'Do you know where you're going to go when you die?' I couldn't get out of that car fast enough."

Schiano is talking now about "it wasn't what I thought it would be" moments. We all have them. As I look around at the suits and business casuals in the room I know they have them. I know I have them.

His moment was in 1994 after Penn State won the Rose Bowl. "I had just had my greatest moment as a professional, and I went back to the hotel and had too much to drink. I woke up the next morning hungover, and it was raining in L.A. I was sitting on the bus and I just started sweating. If you've ever had too much to drink one night, you realize with a hangover you just start sweating for no reason."

Schiano would leave Penn State for the Chicago Bears, where he would serve first as a defensive assistant and then as a defensive backfield coach from 1996 to 1998. In Chicago he would meet special teams coach Danny Abramowicz, who as an NFL player made his mark as a gritty overachiever.

"Danny always beat me into the office, and nobody ever beat me into the office," Schiano remembers. "But instead of looking at film on those mornings, he always had his Bible open."

Schiano would also meet John Maurer in Chicago, a team chaplain who would become a close friend and would come with him to Rutgers.

"Maurer always had a smile on his face and would always say hello when he walked by my office. As a Jersey guy this made me uncomfortable," he says. "I wondered 'Why is this guy being so nice to me?' "

Eventually Maurer and Schiano began having lunch together and then jogging together. Finally, Maurer and Abramowitz shared a tape with him that would change his life.

"I was a coach who had always done whatever it took," he says. "I would do anything to climb the ladder, and if that meant boozing with high school coaches or going to strip clubs with them to get a recruit then so be it. I sacrificed my family. But I learned that all of those things were crutches.

"It started to hit home to me that I was climbing the wrong ladder. I listened to this tape by Bill McCartney from Promise Keepers every night on the way home, for three weeks straight. At the end there was always a call to trust Jesus Christ with your life, but I always fast-forwarded through that part.

"There were no fireworks and no bright lights," says Schiano of his conversion experience. "In fact, we got fired again shortly thereafter, which is becoming a common theme."

After his Chicago firing, Schiano would interview with Butch Davis at Miami for the defensive coordinator position, one that he held from 1999 to 2000.

"We talked for six hours straight in Butch's office, and we rarely talked about football," he says. "We talked about family,

God, philosophies on parenting and coaching kids. And before I left that day he offered me the job."

During his tenure in Miami, the Hurricanes posted a 20–5 record, including an 11–1 record, the No. 2 national ranking and the Sugar Bowl championship in 2000. However, Schiano would experience his lowest professional moment coaching at Miami, losing a heartbreaker to his former mentor, Joe Paterno, at Penn State.

"It was pouring down rain, and we were in control the whole day," he says. "I remember looking across the field at Joe and remembering that he kind of looks like a wet rat when it's raining. His hair is all matted down, and his glasses are all fogged up. I thought I had him. Towards the end of the game I called a blitz that we had just put in that week and hadn't used all day. Danny Morgan, my great middle linebacker, ran into the defensive tackle and was a split-second late getting through, and their quarterback threw a perfect strike for a touchdown. I was devastated. I had never felt so low, and I was asking questions like 'God, why did you let that happen to me?' And I remember getting back to the locker room and emptying out the pockets in my slacks. I found a message there from Dave Wannstedt, who later said he had just, for some reason, felt compelled to call me that morning. The message read 'In the most crucial situation, make the most basic call.'"

Schiano, who grew up in Wyckoff, New Jersey, and graduated from Ramapo High School, took over as the twenty-seventh head coach of the nation's oldest college football program on December 1, 2000. At the press conference, Schiano proclaimed his vision of excellence for Rutgers football. "This program will be built on a rock foundation," he said. "It will take longer than building it on stilts, but when it's built, it will be built forever. This is where I started; this is where I was striving to get back to. I'm thrilled to be here. It's time."

This kind of rhetoric is common at first-day press conferences, and it can be translated to read: "We're going to take our time recruiting the right people, and not bringing in a bunch of JUCO thugs, and it might take some patience, but we're going to get it done."

Several Scarlet Knights have matriculated to the NFL under Schiano's watch, including tight end L. J. Smith who was the starting tight end for the Philadelphia Eagles in Super Bowl XXXVIIII and caught a TD pass. Gary Brackett started at middle linebacker for the Indianapolis Colts throughout the 2005 and 2006 seasons, where he won his first Super Bowl ring.

This season, Leonard captured the "academic" Heisman by winning the Draddy Trophy, while sophomore tailback Ray Rice was one of three finalists for the Maxwell Award, given annually to the nation's top player. Rice also earned Second-Team All-American by the *Associated Press*, Walter Camp Football Foundation and Rivals.com and finished seventh in the voting for the Heisman Trophy. In addition, junior defensive tackle Eric Foster garnered First Team All-America accolades from the Football Writers Association of America.

At the beginning, however, Schiano was, in his words, "falling apart."

"I made a big mistake in that I tried to do it alone," he says. "I was all alone, spiritually. For the first time in my career I didn't have a mentor like a Butch Davis or a John Maurer around."

Maurer, after a stint on the mission field in Kazakhstan, would answer Schiano's call and join his friend at Rutgers where he still serves.

"It took a freshman named William Beckford to wake me up," Schiano says. "Beckford came to me midway through his freshman year and said, 'We need to start praying as a team.' I had sat and prayed in Beckford's living room with him during recruiting and told him that God was going to be a part of this program."

What people have really come to hear, though, are stories about the dream season, and the win over Louisville. Schiano though, says he remembers nothing about that game.

"I went home and watched it on television like I was a fan," he says of that sleepless night. "I don't remember any of the calls I made. I truly had nothing to do with that game."

Whether Schiano is being unnecessarily humble or the Man Upstairs actually had something to do with that game, we'll never know. What we do know, though, are that there are 1,000 people in the room who expect Schiano to keep winning. "God said 'You're not supposed to leave,' " he tells the assembled throng, of his decision to stay in their backyard.

"But I'm smart enough to know that when you lose, nobody wants you to come near them."

CHAPTER 5

THE REGENERATOR:
DANNY WUERFFEL

"THE WORD *became flesh . . . and moved into the neighborhood."* John 1:14 (MSG)

The platitudes happen as often as there happens to be a football game in the Katrina-torn city of New Orleans. "This city has rallied around this team" is the sentiment expressed weekly by the guy in the blazer, holding the microphone. Or, "This team has rallied around this city. This team, just by showing up and playing football, and occasionally scoring more points than the other team, has done so much for the collective morale of New Orleans."

LSU was lauded for winning the Sugar Bowl. Reggie Bush was lauded for just showing up in town and collecting his millions.

Football, they say, has been the great balm in Gilead. It is, of course, just talk, as football doesn't remove mold-borne viruses, or extricate tree branches from the side of one's home. Football is always, at its very best, just a very compelling distraction.

Danny Wuerffel's own home was flooded to the roof when Katrina hit, causing the 1996 Heisman Trophy winner to relocate his wife and child to his hometown of Destin, Florida. He returned, however, to search the streets of New Orleans in the wake of the storm, looking for the children of the Desire Street Academy, where Wuerffel is now employed. Many of the kids, from New Orleans' tough 9th ward neighborhood, were now, literally, on the streets.

Since 1990, Desire Street Ministries has served the impoverished Desire neighborhood within New Orleans' 9th Ward with social outreach programs that meet the residents' specific needs. In the church, there is a buzzword for this called living "incarnationally." But for Danny Wuerffel and the rest of the staff, it is about revitalizing the community through spiritual development, and by meeting the tangible needs of its people.

Even before Hurricane Katrina, one could have made the argument that as urban areas go, New Orleans was one of the most at-risk in the country. And Desire is one of the city's most desperately poor areas. According to the desirestreet.org Web site, "This area of land began as a swamp, was later used as a garbage dump, and during the twentieth century became home to thousands of poor African-American migrant families. In the 1960s, the federal government spent millions of dollars trying to improve the neighborhood by creating one of the nation's largest tracts of subsidized housing. Later, drug use, poverty, and unemployment rates in the neighborhood were the highest in New Orleans, and the physical conditions of the housing project had fallen into such disrepair that it was officially declared unfit for human habitation."

Not exactly the neighborhood you want your son moving into, if your son happens to be a former NFL player, Heisman winner, and overall Great American. "Giving back" for pro athletes typically means a nonprofit foundation, a black-tie gala once a year, and a board of directors. Not living in a neighborhood that was never reached by the American Dream.

"We literally lost everything we had," he says, of the Katrina aftermath. "In a lot of ways I'd be lying if I said it wasn't the worst year of my life, but it's also been a really good, and rich, year spiritually."

Wuerffel, who had every opportunity to hit the banquet circuit and be, as erstwhile banqueteer Paul Hornung says, "on scholarship" for the rest of his life, now splits his time between the Desire Street office in Destin, and New Orleans, where he is working to raise funds and rebuild the Desire Street Academy, also decimated by the storm.

"There were a lot of heroes in the wake of Katrina," he remembers. "We had volunteers with Desire Street T-shirts on just walking through the shelters in hopes of kids seeing the T-shirts and recognizing us.

"There was one incident where one of our board members, wearing a Desire Street T-shirt, was standing by the side of the road on his cell phone, and one of our kids recognized him and jumped out of the car he was in."

Wuerffel and the Desire Street staff found eighty-five of their kids and relocated them to Florida, giving them a second chance at education and, more importantly, hope. The Desire Street Academy, which used to serve 190 students in New Orleans, reopened with eighty at a satellite campus in Florida. Since Katrina, the school has reopened its doors in Baton Rouge.

The academy began with modest goals—to get kids, even temporarily, out of an urban environment pockmarked with severely underperforming schools, in which the class valedictorian was often unable to come up with a passing grade on the ACT. Enter the Desire Street Academy, launched in 2002, "to transform the Desire community by training students to pursue excellence in academics, athletics and the arts in a Christian context."

"These kids suffer from a lack of opportunity, obviously, but that's only part of the solution," Wuerffel says. "Most of them start out bright eyed, smiling kids and then as the years go by you see the realities of life—the disintegration of the family—kill all sense of hope in their lives. It's a really sad thing."

I can tell that Wuerffel isn't terribly interested in talking about football. He doesn't once mention the Heisman Trophy, and, at least at first, I intentionally don't ask. I feel as though I should wonder what became of the actual trophy—whether it was swept away by hurricane waters or whether it sits on a mantel in his parents' home. He is not, in the traditional Deep South sense, a "football guy"—one who eats, sleeps, and breathes the sport on a daily basis.

Wuerffel broke numerous records at the University of Florida and many in the NCAA during his career at UF. He was the first college athlete to win the Heisman and Draddy (for the NCAA student-athlete of the year) trophies in a single season (1996). He also won four consecutive SEC titles between 1993 and 1996, and the 1996 National Championship in a statement victory (52–20) over archrival Florida State University at the 1997 Sugar Bowl in New Orleans. He describes himself as a "competitor" but says he rarely has pangs of jealousy, or a desire to play football again. Though he admits to "feeling it" when the Gators beat Ohio State in the Fiesta Bowl this season.

"My buddy Trent [Dilfer] is a football guy in that he loves every aspect of it," he says. "But there are a lot of things about it that I'm glad I don't have to deal with now."

Wuerffel is one of those athletes whose charisma is probably best enjoyed by just watching him play the game—that is, he is not one to sit for hours spinning knee-slapping yarns about old teammates and their past glories.

On that night against Florida State, in the 1997 Sugar Bowl, it all may have come together for Wuerffel in the sense that he led his team to victory in what is too often called a "statement" game. The Florida State defense was loaded with NFL draft choices including Reinard Wilson, Andre Wadsworth, and Peter Boulware; and they had been criticized during the week by Spurrier, who insisted that the Seminoles made a habit of hitting Wuerffel late in their last meeting. It was equal parts motivational ploy (see bulletin board material), television hype, and some reality mixed in for good measure. But the truth is, when one thinks of paragons of self-control and no-nonsense play, neither of these schools really come to mind.

"Danny is one of those New Testament fellas, after he's slapped upside the head he turns the other cheek and says 'Lord forgive them for they know not what they do,' " Spurrier explained at a news conference, in a rare display of biblical scholarship. "I'm more of an Old Testament guy myself," he said. "You spear me in the head I'm gonna spear you back."

Wuerffel's offense was loaded with stars as well—including Jacquez Green, Ike Hilliard, Fred Taylor, and Zach Piller, who would go on to have a long career as an NFL left tackle. On the season, Wuerffel had passed for over 3,600 yards and tossed 39 TDs as opposed to only 13 picks. Even in 1997, there was a certain creativity about Steve Spurrier's offense. Many of the formations and sets he employed then are seen now, as the shotgun spread offense is currently the flavor of the month in college football.

It is also somewhat astonishing, watching film of this game, the number of very good college players for these marquee programs who had nothing in the way of a significant NFL career. Wayne Messam. Daryl Bush. Dan Kendra. Thad Busby. And a creatively named, 286-pound fullback named Pooh Bear Williams. You just hope they all got their degrees.

Wuerffel is, of course, sensational in the game, making throw after accurate throw, often off his back foot, or just before being smacked in the facemask by a furious Florida State rush. Backpedaling, he hits Ike Hilliard in the second quarter on a textbook post route versus single coverage. On the same drive, under pressure, he throws back across his body, hitting Fred Taylor who gets knocked out of bounds just before crossing the end zone stripe. Taylor will score on the next play.

On what is, era-wise, the cusp of a cultural shift, Wuerffel offers little in the way of celebration. To myself celebrate this as "old-school" or "refreshing" would be a horrible cliche but I can't help doing so. Wuerffel was 13–22 for 246 yards and two scores with 5:18 left in the first half. It had the beginnings of a beatdown.

Wuerffel throws his third TD pass to Ike Hilliard on a slant, midway through the third quarter. Once again, he does so with the rush in his face and, once again, is knocked down. Wuerffel, in fact, ends an astonishing number of plays on his back.

Danny's father, John Wuerffel, an Air Force chaplain, is interviewed by Lynn Swann on the sideline. "It worries you," he says of the hits that his son has taken during the course of the ballgame. "It's too many hits. It's too often. You get worried he's not going to walk away . . . it scares you."

Wuerffel evades a pass rush and runs the football in for a score of his own, with thirteen seconds remaining in the third quarter. The score comes out of a shotgun formation, where all of his wide receivers, in addition to the two running backs, are lined up to his left. He takes the ball and simply runs to the right side of the field which is largely vacant. The extra point makes it 38–20 Florida, and the game is effectively over.

At the game's conclusion, the reporters, cameramen, and ABC's Lynn Swann all swirl around Wuerrfel and his coach.

"I have to give all glory and praise to Jesus Christ my Lord and Savior," he says. "It's been a wonderful career. So many great friends and so many great moments. This is one of the best. Defense, offense, special teams, punt team, everybody played their best tonight and we're just real excited."

Swann goes on to call Wuerffel a "great asset to college football" and "an inspiration for young people."

Wuerrfel is unusually articulate and reflective for a kid his age, so the "aw-shucks" nature of the interview is seen less as contrived and more as just the genuine end of, perhaps, a more innocent era. In a short time both Wuerrfel and his coach would be receiving beatings at the NFL level.

By the world's standards, Wuerffel's pro career could probably be characterized as a disappointment, or at least very pedestrian. Wuerffel spent six seasons as a backup quarterback with New Orleans, Green Bay, and Washington.

In six seasons, Wuerffel completed 184 of 350 passes, with 12 touchdowns and 22 interceptions. He also spent one season in NFL Europe. He is perhaps best remembered for his link to Steve Spurrier, his college coach, who would go on to coach him with the Washington Redskins. Spurrier was summarily panned in the media for his performance as an NFL coach, and has since returned to the SEC as head coach of the South Carolina Gamecocks.

"I can honestly say that Coach Spurrier is the most hands-on coach I've ever been around," he says. "There's nothing 'background' or 'administrative' about him, and he has an incredible attention to detail. He scrutinized everything from your footwork to the way your shoulders were turned, and we had patterns where he'd say, 'I need you to put it three yards outside the numbers, at 22 yards, and if you don't put it there it won't work.' But he also had, at the same time, a sort of 'draw up a play in the dirt' and 'if they're doing that, we're gonna do this' kind of attitude.'"

Wuerffel cites a "tough" ownership situation in Washington (an understatement, to be sure, regarding the heavily involved Daniel Snyder) and a cavalier attitude toward the running game as possible reasons for his coach's failure, but is slow to criticize Spurrier, whom he admires. He also blames a "win now" attitude and general lack of patience at the next level.

"There's an instability about life in the NFL," he says. "There are only a handful of guys that are sure they're going to have a spot on the roster, and even when you're sure you're never really sure. When you're single, I guess, that's fine, but it's really tough to ask your family to move year in and year out."

Wuerrfel moved his young family thirteen times in his first four years of marriage. Such is the unsettled life of an NFL journeyman. And he is routinely seen on lists with players like Andre Ware, Gino Torretta, Eric Crouch, and Charlie Ward as Heisman winners who "flopped" at the NFL level.

"But then there were things you just tried to enjoy," he continues, "like being on the sideline and watching Brett Favre throw passes. There were times when I just thought to myself 'wow, it's great to be here.' Beating Peyton Manning on his home field was a thrill . . . but by and large being a backup quarterback is a little bit boring. You really don't get a chance to use all of your creative faculties.

"I probably use more creativity here than I did when I was a football player," he says from the office in Destin, where they have already dealt with a computer crash, among other issues this week. "One day I might be going to the academy to work out and play basketball with the guys, and then the next day I'm giving a talk to executives and trying to raise money. It's ever-changing. But you know what? I love being 'interrupted' by the kids. I'll sit down at my desk, ready to do something, and the kids will come by and want to hang out. I like that.

"I suppose I might have liked to have been a fighter pilot," Wuerffel says, when I ask him what he might have been had football not been a factor. "I've had the chance to ride in some F-16s and I really enjoyed it. But my first love was basketball. My goal as a ninth grader was to get a college scholarship and I really thought it was going to be in basketball. But then I realized there aren't many 6-foot-2 power forwards in college ball, and I could throw a football pretty well so it just kind of worked out."

There is false humility, and there is real humility, and I suppose most sportswriters can tell the difference, having been around both for much of their careers. I ask Wuerffel, finally, about the process by which he, a white guy with all of the opportunities in the world to eat banquet food and be made much of, chose his current life.

"It was just slow steps," he says, of his decision to work in the Ninth Ward. "Coming out of college, because of my faith and how it was changing me, I wanted to be a part of something in the inner city. Not out of a feeling of obligation, but because I wanted to. So I decided as my NFL career was winding down that I would continue to train for football, but go to work part-time for Desire Street. Every day, driving in, I would turn right to go and work out, or turn left to go the office. As the days went by it just kept getting harder to turn right."

It's no secret that college football is big business. According to an ESPN.com report, Texas earned a reported $42 million profit from football during the '05–'06 fiscal year. Michigan earned approximately $37 million, while Florida earned $32 million during that same period. The money, of course, comes from television, marketing rights, and the luxury boxes that make the college stadiums that used to be quaint look a lot like their NFL counterparts.

There was a full hour of pregame National Championship festivities on Fox this season, in which a field-size flag was unfurled, and a variety of celebrities gave their opinions on the upcoming game. In a final flourish, a bald eagle flew the length of the stadium, further cementing the link between football, corporate America, and patriotism. All for a game that would be decided by the play of eighteen- to twenty-one-year-olds. Like all great American sporting events, the National Championship has become a parody of itself.

"There are aspects of college football where it retains the whole 'preparing young men for life' and 'teaching a work ethic' and that sort of thing," Wuerffel says. "But too often—at least these days—it seems like big business gets it off track a little bit.

"I felt like there wasn't a whole lot of time for other activities," Wuerffel recalls, of his time as a football god at the University of Florida. "But at the same time I was able to focus enough on my studies and be involved in other things. They try hard to protect the student part of 'student athlete.' "

It's strange that after a decorated high school career—Wuerffel attended Fort Walton Beach Senior High School, leading the Vikings to an undefeated season as a senior while winning the Florida AAAA state football championship in 1991—and the college accolades, that he has so soon been relegated to the category of "whatever happened to . . . ?" He doesn't often appear on behalf of the University, and isn't the type of alum to stalk sidelines for "face time" during the bowl extravaganzas. He reflects, finally, on what it is that he appreciates most about college football.

"The beauty of the sport," he says, "is that you get eighty guys together with so many different backgrounds. These are guys with no reason to like each other, and every reason not to—country rednecks, guys from the inner city, guys from the suburbs—and when people have a common goal they pull together and develop some of the most incredible friendships."

CHAPTER 6

THE ONLY ALL-STAR GAME THAT MATTERS:
THE SENIOR BOWL, JANUARY 29

"YOU WITH THE PANTHERS?" says a deep, Southern-tinged voice as I step out of my hotel room and into the hallway at the Riverview Plaza Hotel in Mobile, Alabama. The voice is covered head-to-toe in expensive Under Armour swag—hat, sweatshirt, sweatpants, and backpack—tipping me off that he is a player, Kevin Kolb, a quarterback from the University of Houston. Kolb passed for more than 12,000 yards and 85 touchdowns in thirty-six starts. He has been compared, at times, to Brett Favre. Kolb, today, wants to know whether I am worth talking to.

At the Senior Bowl, held annually in Mobile, it's all about two things: your badge and your swag. There is a distinct pecking order in place here, at the NFL's de facto annual convention. Team reps, like scouts and coaches, wear team-issued gear, reminding players who have been the property of one place (a university) that they will soon be the highly paid property of another (an NFL squad). These team reps troll the lobby, dispensing questionnaires to players (would you rather be a cat or a dog?) and conducting on-the-spot interviews. The players themselves, each clad in over two-hundred-dollars' worth of Under Armour gear, are next on the food chain. They walk, slope-shouldered, through lobbies, down hallways, and in and out of meeting rooms. The world is their oyster now—most of them will be millionaires, barring injury, in the span of a few short months. They talk and laugh, loudly, in groups. They huddle in corners with their agents, who are next on the food chain, no doubt devising ways to spend large amounts of money. Contrary to popular belief, the agents don't sport horns and a tail, nor are many of them the slimeballs they are made out to be (though some are). They simply wait in the second-floor lobby for clients, or potential clients, to come through. Some are here to peddle the wares of players who left college a couple of years ago—their slim prospects becoming even slimmer as the days go by.

The bottom-dwellers in this scene, though, are the autograph hounds. Autograph hounds used to be children with stars in their eyes, using the autograph as a chance to get close to their favorite, larger-than-life athlete. Now, they are paunchy, ill-kempt, thirty-something eBay mavens, relegated to a chilly corner of the adjacent parking garage, where they stand with bags and boxes full of memorabilia—helmets, jerseys, T-shirts, photos—waiting for the signature that will raise the value of the item immeasurably and take it from being just a piece of replica plastic, to a piece of replica plastic bearing the signature of Troy Smith or Drew Stanton. They fix their eyes on you as you exit the hotel and walk through the ramp. They read your badge (is he a player?) and study your face. And then, when they realize you are nobody, they turn away, completely disgusted.

Senior Bowl practices, conducted on the Field Turf at Ladd-Peebles Stadium, are where the majority of the talent-evaluation takes place. The stadium itself is nestled into an old working-class Mobile neighborhood, just past a couple of cemeteries. The stadium is not un-nice; it is just an old, metal hulk. There is a little bit of rust visible. It is the only element of the week that doesn't fit with Under Armour's space-age ethos, which seems to be "our clothes will send you to the moon, and you'll look really sexy in the process."

The practice setting is a who's who of NFL dignitaries. GMs and scouts from various teams scatter throughout the West stands, constantly chattering about players and their prospects. As is typical in the Deep South, the stadium is surrounded by a hedgerow, and I am met there by Marv Levy, Harvard graduate, author, multiple Super Bowl coach, and current GM of the Buffalo Bills. He has just arrived in town. He looks like your grandfather might, wearing a windbreaker and an NFL 75 ballcap that dates back to exactly 1994. The cap has a flat bill. Levy, however, is charming. I ask him about this year's crop of players.

"I'm just getting familiar with them," he says. "I'm not one of these GMs that flies all over the country during the college season looking at guys. The way I see it is that we have a staff for that . . . but then I like to sit down with all of the tapes and break things down. That's what I'll do for the next two or three months."

"Sounds like fun," I say to Levy, sincerely. Though writing is fulfilling, I'll never lose the desire to be a part of a team, and talent-evaluation is something I've always enjoyed.

"There are some days when I say to myself 'this is really boring' " he says, honestly. "But most days, yeah, it is really fun."

Speaking of, in the corner of the field the South quarterbacks

(Kolb, Jordan Palmer, and Chris Leak) are trying to see who can throw a football out of the stadium and through one of the gates in the South end zone stands. The contest is the brainchild of 49ers assistant coach Norv Turner, who has been the subject of rumors all week, as he is a candidate for the vacant Dallas Cowboys head coaching position. These are the games that the athletically prodigious play to entertain the rest of us, who would probably be hard-pressed to throw a football accurately from one end of our office to the other. The quarterbacks each take a drop, and then launch a football (probably worth about seventy-five bucks apiece) into the bleachers. Palmer, the 6-foot-5-inch brother of Cincinnati Bengals QB Carson Palmer, is the first to complete the task, drawing jokes about per diem bets from his counterparts. Despite Leak's newly minted National Championship, Palmer is considered the cream of the South team's quarterbacking crop. He has the all-important measurables—a rocket arm, height, and a winning pedigree. Palmer holds all of UTEP's career passing and total offense records and started thirty-six straight games. Leak, on the other hand, looks almost slight by comparison. He is listed at a generous 6-foot and 210 pounds, however, he looks more like 190 on the field. Still though, his competitiveness and mobility shine though. And he shows touch on deep balls, throwing a ball that the South receivers describe as "catchable."

Leak was one of a handful of college quarterbacks who left the high school ranks with a Heisman Trophy as an almost foregone conclusion (see Ron Powlus). Instead, Leak never won a Heisman and despite numerous honors (BCS National Championship MVP, All-SEC recognition, etc.) never garnered the affection of fans like Florida's only other National Championship quarterback, Danny Wuerffel.

Chris Leak has gone from being a National Champion just a few weeks ago to being the quarterback here with the most to prove, as he is being projected, at best, as a day-two draft choice.

I speak with him on his way off the field. His large, round eyes show the telltale signs of fatigue, and he sounds completely exhausted.

Around the fence, there are hopefuls of all kinds. There are a few recognizable agents, but by and large there are thirty-somethings with leather jackets, cell phones attached to their ears, and sunglasses, hoping to embody the look that they think a sports-agent should embody. Their badges are emblazoned with names of companies you've probably never heard of, and probably never will—usually starting with a word like "momentum" or "elite" and always ending in the word "sports." They are outnumbered only by the guys who run draft Web sites—most of whom are overweight and underathletic, but spend their days writing about how so-and-so is a step slow, and so-and-so can't throw the deep out. They are, in a figurative sense, Mel Kiper's legion of bastard children.

Still, though, there are players with sweatshirts that read TORONTO ARGONAUTS and GREEN BAY BOMBERS. They have the same athletic builds and swagger as the twenty-one-year-olds on the field, but they are minor leaguers, like Aaron Pruitt, from Glendale College, here with the hopes of running into an NFL scout or executive who can turn their lives around.

Pruitt, who is bright and articulate, last played in a professional indoor league, and has an agent from the Mobile area, who brought him down here. There is a maturity about him that only comes from life experiences. The kids on the field, no matter how polished, don't have it.

"People are opening their options," he says of scouts and their opinions of minor leaguers like himself. "Their eyes and ears are open to any new talent that they can see."

Pruitt tells me that his last college season was 2004, making it three years since he last played the outdoor game. He has a job working with his trainer, and also has a part-time job at Pizza Hut, to provide for his wife and daughter.

Florida State linebacker Buster Davis looks even shorter in real life than he does on the field. Davis, the sawed-off MLB who was the object of Coach Mike Singletary's scorn today on the field, is lounging in a pair of sweats and brand-new Timberland boots. Davis, I notice, is the only player not availing himself to the scads of Under Armour gear being worn by his teammates. One gets the impression that Davis is the kind of guy who keeps things real, whatever that means. He is chatty, and honest.

"I don't really care what they do," he says, when he is asked by another guy who the Seminoles hired to replace their offensive coordinator. After some conversation with the other guy, who turns out to be a sports agent, it becomes apparent that the guy doesn't know who Davis is, or that he is a player. Behind us, on the obligatory big-screen television showing a *Groundhog Day*–esque loop of NFL Network programming, Davis can be seen in a replay of the day's practice. He watches his moves closely.

"So who do you coach for?" asks the guy. Davis, obviously miffed, replies, "I play. I'm a player." The other man is undeterred, and has come armed with the kind of boozy confidence you often see in hotel lobbies. He could be any salesman, from anywhere.

Davis was an early-week victim of another Senior Bowl tradition, the weigh-in, in which players are stripped to their skivvies and made to stand on a podium while upwards of 750 scouts, media, and random onlookers scrutinize their physique and body dimensions. These scouts will then scribble things like "has a weightlifter's build" or "skinny legs" or "a little doughy." It is a little ironic that perhaps nowhere in the world could a more testosterone-driven, heterosexual crowd be found (football coaches, scouts), yet the highlight of their week is sitting in a ballroom, looking at nearly naked men. It just speaks to the gravity of the financial commitments made to these players. If a player has a weakness, it will be discovered this week.

Davis's weakness just happened to be that he measured closer to 5-foot-8 than the 5-foot-10 he is credited with in the Florida State media guide. This is not news, however, as media guides are famous for this. Other players such as Leak, the Florida QB, and Brian Leonard (weighed 224 instead of the advertised 238) have fallen victim to the scales as well. Davis, though, seems to be taking the disappointment in stride, and hasn't let it dampen his enthusiasm about his own game.

"It doesn't bother me one bit," Davis told *Pro Football Weekly*, when asked about his size. "Me, personally, I think I've outplayed that height stuff. That shouldn't have anything to do with it because, as you can see, I can play ball regardless of how tall I am. There are some 6-foot-2 guys out there that can't play half as good as me. I think it's a joke, really, every time somebody brings it up.

"I definitely think I'm a first-round-type player," he says. "I've probably improved my stock more than anybody down here, but I think all of the guys in our group are first or second round type guys. Not to give myself too much credit but I think I might be a little shorter version of Ray Lewis." Davis goes on to add that it is his dream to play next to Ray Lewis, as a Baltimore Raven.

Davis has been grouped with, among others, Patrick Willis (Ole Miss), and Earl Everett (Florida). His group, this week, is being coached by NFL Hall of Famer Mike Singletary, himself a former linebacker and leader of the Chicago Bears "Monsters of the Midway" defense in the late eighties. Singletary, who is at least as fit as he was as a player, has been merciless in his instruction of the All-Stars. He was especially rough on Davis in a bag drill this afternoon, in which the linebackers simply shuffled from side to side between bags. Davis lets up a bit before the end of the drill.

"I didn't say stop!" Singletary shouts. Davis is bent over at the waist, attempting to catch his breath. The coach then gets inside of the bags to show the players the proper technique. Singletary thanks the players at the conclusion of the drill, and before moving on to the next.

"The little fella from Florida State," says Singletary after practice, "he reminds me of me a little bit. He wants to take on the world. He's out there fighting for his life. I like all of them. I look at this as an opportunity to help a guy make a team. It's a privilege to come out here and coach these kids—six kids—who I can put my hands on and really try to instill in them something that will help them in training camp."

"It's been a dream come true, working with Coach [Singletary]," Davis says. "It's not often you get to be coached by a Hall of Fame backer. The practices are fast and hard. I thought we practiced fast at Florida State but man . . . this ain't even training camp, you know? If I get drafted by San Francisco I better come into camp at 225!" Davis currently weighs 244 and has a build that can only be described as "compact." In fact, he resembles boxer Mike Tyson in some ways. Davis, after racking up more than 100 tackles and five sacks in addition to two forced fumbles and an interception, was a first-team All-ACC selection, in addition to being named All-American by the American Football Coaches Association. He has recorded 258 career tackles, 25.5 tackles for loss and eight sacks in forty-eight career starts.

Davis ended up playing all three linebacker positions—strong, weakside, and middle—in his career at Florida State, a fact that, he told ESPN, didn't make him happy:

"When I arrived they moved me from ILB to OLB, and I wasn't happy. I was young. I didn't want to hear that. I decided to leave school after two weeks. I only stayed because my mom made me . . . I was a little rebel when I first came here, but now I've totally changed. I pulled a 180. When our team votes you team captain, that's the best thing. That tells you how far I've come."

It's that versatility, however, coupled with Davis's football smarts and aggression, that make him an attractive NFL commodity.

He has solid instincts and never seems to be out of position on film, drawing comparisons to Dexter Coakley, London Fletcher, and Sam Mills.

On the screen, Davis watches himself taking a tongue-lashing from Singletary. He shakes his head, but is proud of his proximity to the Hall of Famer. He simply mutters, "Coach" under his breath, and shakes his head. "My coach worked me hard at Florida State, but never this hard," he says. "When the coaches here say they want something now, they mean right now."

The agent has returned and talk has turned to current NFL players and NFL teams. Davis is asked about the antics of Terrell Owens.

"Who wants to coach a guy like TO?" he asks, rhetorically. "You know what I think? I think he needs someone to bust him in the mouth."

It seems like every ten feet in the Mobile Convention Center or the Riverview Plaza Hotel, there is a flat-screen television showing the NFL Network. Watching their programming is like experiencing déjà vu. All of their shows have the same look and feel, and I often wonder how their talking heads keep from going crazy.

One such talking head, over my right shoulder, is Mike Mayock, talking about Central Michigan tackle Joe Staley ("He really helped himself this week . . . has turned himself into a marquee left tackle after coming into college as a tight end), and Florida State running back Lorenzo Booker ("Would make a great third-down back"). Mayock, who had a cup of coffee as a defensive back with the New York Giants in the early eighties, has ascended near the top of draftdom. He is probably second only to Mel Kiper in terms of exposure, and his opinion matters. The players here are vying for positive attention, something that translates directly into dollars on draft day.

They are also vying for the attention of the head coaches, this year Jon Gruden of the Tampa Bay Buccaneers, and Mike Nolan of the San Francisco 49ers. The two men, gathering for an evening press conference, are a study in opposites. Gruden gets around in a team-issued sweatsuit and ballcap. He has a joke for one of the photographers. He is in his early forties, but looks ten years younger. He looks like a frat guy who may have tormented many, but who because of an outsize dose of charisma, probably has, and may always, get a pass in life. Gruden is easy to like. Neither man, of course, says anything of consequence in these evening pressers: They are, for the most part, extremely boring.

Nolan is a perfect foil for Jon Gruden's fratboy. Nolan appears to be the classic first child—tucked in, buttoned down, all business, all the time. He is thin, high-strung, and dapper—indeed, he was one of two coaches who petitioned the league for the right to wear a suit on the sideline this season. "Short, sweet, and to the point," he says, ascending the podium and looking profoundly bored. He says, interestingly, that none of the players on his squad is NFL-ready. "No draft pick is NFL-ready until he goes through camp," he says, likening NFL rookies to freshmen entering college. Finally, someone asks him about the performance of Buster Davis, the diminutive but confident linebacker from Florida State. I have grown to enjoy Davis, and find myself pulling for him during the practice sessions. Nolan reacts with a blank stare.

"Go by numbers," Nolan says. Somebody replies that Davis is the short guy who wears No. 7. "On film he doesn't play like a little guy."

Almost 4,000 players have participated in the Senior Bowl over the years, with twenty-six of them going on to NFL careers that have ended in the Pro Football Hall of Fame, with notables including Joe Namath, Walter Payton, Bo Jackson, Lynn Swann, and Ray Nitschke among others. Almost 100 more will join that list of Senior Bowl participants on Saturday.

The first Senior Bowl game was played in Jacksonville, Florida, in 1950. Every year since it's been played at Ladd-Peebles Stadium in Mobile, often, it seems in inclement weather.

The 2007 game was conducted in a driving downpour, which resulted in a total of 12 fumbles, and a less than ideal opportunity to view the prospects in action.

The North, led by Heisman Trophy–winner Troy Smith and Penn State running back Tony Hunt, outgained the South 264–93 in total yards, and went on to win by a 27–0 margin in a game that really wasn't as close as the score indicated. It seemed that the South squad rarely progressed past midfield, plagued the entire time by turnovers. Kevin Kolb, my hallmate in the Riverview Plaza, struggled mightily, completing only two passes, and newly minted National Champion Chris Leak managed only 23 yards passing. On the night before the game I was having trouble sleeping, and through the wall could hear Kolb going over his formation and play calls with a coach or a roommate. Stuff like "I-right, slot-right 47 go" and "236 Y-bingo switch." It was the language of football, decipherable only by Kolb and his teammates.

It should be noted, however, that Buster Davis notched 5 total tackles—good for second among all defenders.

Big E is sauntering behind me this morning, on the way to the Convention Center hospitality deck to resume his post as the worldwide spokesman for Under Armour, also known as the company that is taking over the world. Big E's real name is Eric Ogbogu, and in addition to a cup of coffee with the Dallas Cowboys, he was a standout defensive end for the University of Maryland, where he met Under Armour's founder, Kevin Plank. Plank was a college teammate of the sculpted Ogbogu, and ostensibly wanted to design a line of performance apparel that would make him feel like Ogbogu looks.

"Me and the CEO were real good friends in college," he says. "We played on the same football team. The first couple years of the company he just kind of wanted to know if I wanted to do a couple of print ads for him. It went from there and kept growing."

The idea is brilliant in its simplicity—replace the traditional, sweat-soaked, cotton-blend "gray" that players have worn under their pads since the beginning of time, with a shirt that is tight and spandexy. The logic being that the shirt, in addition to looking infinitely cooler than cotton while allowing the players to show off muscles they've spent years of their lives building, also stays lighter when one sweats all over it.

Their "official" blurb is more, well, official:

> . . . the Baltimore based corporation is the originator of moisture-wicking performance apparel worn by athletes, and is a leading developer, marketer, and distributor of branded performance apparel . . . the brand's moisture-wicking fabrications (ed. That's my favorite part . . . sounds like a Don King word) are engineered in many different designs and styles . . . to provide a performance alternative to traditional natural fiber products.

"You have performance tires, performance shoes, why not performance clothes?" asks Big E, rhetorically, when we meet on the balcony. True to form, and like the other players, he is bedecked in the tight, dazzly material, head to toe. There is something space-agey and special about the fabric itself, though I couldn't say what. The back of his performance gray T-shirt reads, WE MUST PROTECT THIS HOUSE, an ambiguously motivating slogan he made famous in Under Armour's first television ad several years ago. This is a good time to admit that if I had any sense at all I would have purchased Under Armour stock the moment I saw Big E's biceps encased in the space-age fibers. I knew this stuff (lingerie for men, according to my wife) would be big.

"I knew it would be successful," says Big E, who also has a large, diamond-encrusted Under Armour medallion dangling from his neck that is probably worth more than the rented, midsize sedan that I drove to Mobile. "People like to feel big and strong, and they think 'I want to be just like him,' " he adds. "You feel great when you wear this stuff."

Under Armour very methodically undertook the task of product placement—being sure to get its logo on to the hottest and most visible entities in sports and entertainment. They were perhaps the most oft-viewed character in ESPN's short-lived and controversial drama, *Playmakers*, where every player spent nearly every waking moment in the gear. Then it was on to locking down college programs—like Maryland and Auburn—who now wear the product, and finally this, the sponsorship of the one Bowl Game in America that truly matters. The crossover between college and the pros.

"I'm hoping to get back into football," says Big E, finally, breaking character for a moment. Ogbogu's clock is ticking, however, as he is thirty-one years old. Oddly, Ogbogu's parents never wanted him to play football in the first place, banning the sport from their home. He played his first two years under a veil of secrecy. "It trips me out to see myself on the billboards and commercials . . . people coming up to me and saying, 'Hey, you look just like that guy from the commercial or the mannequin.' But I really miss playing. This is my first year out of the game." I ask Big E if it is tough for him to be here, at the Senior Bowl, watching other, younger, faster players embarking on what was once his dream. He thinks for a moment.

"I like the looks on their faces," he says. "They're young guys about to live a dream."

CHAPTER 7

THE RECRUITER:
MARK HAGEN, PURDUE UNIVERSITY

THERE IS LESS URGENCY than I thought there would be in the lobby of the downtown Lansing Radisson Inn on the morning of November 4. The Purdue Boilermakers are in town to play the Michigan State Spartans, and I have to think that the hotel selection was intentional—the Boilers are staying a good five miles away from campus and the bars, clubs and mayhem that accompany a weekend in a Big Ten town.

The lobby itself is serene. There are a few cheerleaders in sweatpants and no makeup slumped over the stuffed leather chairs in the lobby reading books like *Introductory Physics* and *Literature for Life*. I am reminded that they will one day have a purpose in life beyond looking perky.

There is also an abundance of team-issued apparel present. The occasional coach steps sleepily off the elevator, outfitted head-to-toe in Purdue Nike apparel. The licensing contracts afforded Big Ten programs by their outfitters is extensive, and one gets the impression that a coach never has to worry about what he's wearing. The idea of packing one's own casual clothing for this occasion seems ludicrous. The days of Bear Bryant in a plaid sport jacket and fedora are long gone—now, that sport jacket would have to bear a Nike swoosh, and the fedora would be "officially licensed."

Purdue head coach Joe Tiller has entered the lobby, alone, and is walking around somewhat aimlessly, looking for a newspaper. He stops briefly by my chair to pick up a copy of my first book, *Facing Tyson,* which I have brought for Mark Hagen, his assistant coach and recruiting coordinator.

"I'm not crazy about playing the late games," says Hagen, who has joined me in the lobby. "There's nothing to do in the morning. I'd rather just roll out of bed and play."

Hagen, in fact, has the look of a coach who could still play. He is in his mid-thirties, and looks to have the same dimensions he had as an All-Big Ten linebacker at Indiana. Hagen was a four-year letter-winner, two-time second team All-Big Ten selection (1990 and 1991) and three-time Academic All-Big Ten honoree (1989, 1990, and 1991). He returned an interception 21 yards for a touchdown against Purdue in West Lafayette on November 24, 1990. Hagen was the 1991 Copper Bowl Most Valuable Defensive Player (11 tackles in a 24–0 victory over Baylor) and the team's Balfour Award recipient in 1991 for bringing distinction and honor to the university.

I remind him that he recruited me in 1994 when I was coming out of high school, and showed my dad around the Indiana facilities on a cold day in November. I can tell he has no recollection of the event.

"Many years ago," he says. "I was doing football operations back then, for Coach [Bill] Mallory."

Rutgers fullback Brian Leonard executes the now-famous
"Leonard Leap."

Central Michigan All-American DE Dan Bazuin awaits a play early in the 2006 season.

Heisman Trophy winner Danny Wuerffel and members of the Desire Street Academy football team.

Former Michigan State linebacker Charlie "Mad Dog" Thornhill.

Embattled Taylor University head coach James Bell signals in a play from the sidelines.

First-round prospect Joe Staley executes the vertical jump in front of a room full of NFL scouts.

Staley in pass protection, early in the 2006 season.

Former Michigan State star and NFL veteran Herb Haygood in the low minors, as a member of the Battle Creek (MI) Crunch.

Grand Valley State's Cullen Finnerty: the winningest quarterback in NCAA history.

ESPN draft guru Todd McShay, the heir-apparent to Mel Kiper.

He does, though, ask where I'd gone to school, and how my football career played out. About my family. If I make it back to Indiana much. He has the personality and charm requisite of a head coach these days, when coaches can no longer be dour, gruff geniuses but must engage the public on a regular basis.

"I'm originally from Carmel," he says. "I went to Northern Illinois with Joe Novak, who was the defensive coordinator at Indiana when you were being recruited. I did football operations for Coach Mallory at Indiana, after working as a GA [graduate assistant] in the weight room. I spent four years at Northern Illinois during some of their lean years, when we were just trying to get the program on track."

Hagen is in his eighth season at Purdue after being hired March 28, 2000. He is in his fifth year as special teams coordinator and third as assistant head coach. In addition, he is in his second season working with the linebackers after coaching the defensive tackles for six seasons.

From 2000 to 2004, the Boilermakers ranked third, third, fourth, third, and second in the Big Ten in rushing defense, yielding 149.8, 126.9, 116.2, 96.4, and 105.3 yards per game. They were 46th in the nation in 2000, 34th in 2001, 23rd in 2002, 10th in 2003, and 14th in 2004.

One of Hagen's pupils, Matt Mitrione, was named first-team All-Big Ten in 2001 and played one season with the New York Giants. Another, Craig Terrill, was a sixth-round draft pick of the Seattle Seahawks in 2004.

Hagen's effect on special teams was notable as well. The Boilermakers went from 109th in the nation in kickoff returns in 2002 (17.5 average) to 46th in 2003 (21.1) and from 69th in punt returns in 2002 (9.2) to 46th in 2003 (10.4). At the same time, kicker Ben Jones tied the Big Ten season record with 25 field goals.

I ask Hagen about the toll the coaching life takes on his family, whom he mentions often. Road trips like these, away from the family, when one would normally be puttering around the yard or tossing a ball with the kids, are a prime example.

"Tough. You have to have a family that's very understanding," he says. "In retrospect I think my wife Denise was prepped a little bit as a kid, because her dad was a high school basketball coach in Indiana. The time commitment is extreme during the season. You don't see them a lot so you have to make the time count, and maximize every minute you have with them. I'd be lying if I said it was easy . . . but there are people in the corporate world who are on the road all the time."

Hagen also serves in a recruiting capacity at Purdue as the instate and Chicago-area coordinator, and I am fascinated by the challenges of recruiting potential players to a solid, but not elite Big Ten program. Going into the November 4 game, Purdue was sitting at 5–4, and was coming off losses to Wisconsin and Penn State. Purdue is nestled in the Northwest Indiana countryside in West Lafayette, not exactly a hot destination point for blue chip, inner-city recruits—specifically speedsters from the Deep South.

"Along with Northwestern, Purdue is the only other school in the Big Ten that doesn't offer a general studies or a university studies type of major," he says. General studies being the major that is often massaged to breeze athletes through a given system, keeping them happy, eligible, and focused on football. "So whichever major you get into you're going to compete. And I think the Big Ten is a leader in academics, but Purdue and Northwestern take it even a step further.

"So we need to find a student athlete who has a commitment to academics . . . somebody who will get up and go to class. We try to sell wide receivers based on our scheme—the fact that we throw the ball a lot. That's very appealing to receivers and quarterbacks and we think we can get in on some big guys just based on our offensive philosophy. We've had great success putting defensive ends in the NFL, so that's a natural tie in and selling point," he says. Hagen has another premier defensive end this sea-son in Anthony Spencer, who will soon join former Boilermaker teammates Ray Edwards and Rob Ninkovich in the NFL.

"But to be honest, we're going to lose more blue-chip battles than we're going to win going head-to-head with Michigan, Ohio State, and Penn State. You have to go after some diamonds in the rough. What we go after is speed. We're going to go after a high school safety who runs well but doesn't have great speed, with a good frame and make a linebacker out of him. We'll grab a tall, rangy high school TE and make him a tackle. You have to get cre-ative and project where a guy might be best utilized.

"We've had a great deal of success recruiting down in Texas, and the thing you realize there is that football is important to them," he says. "And that's basically the main question we ask, and need to find out about a person during the process: How im-portant is football in his life? There's so much going on out there, and there's so much for a kid to do, sometimes on a pecking order football isn't a high priority for a lot of these guys."

On Rivals.com one can view no less than twenty-five photos of young Jimmy Clausen, the spiky-haired phenom who has given a "strong verbal" commitment to Notre Dame. One can also, at the moment, for a fee view twenty-nine videos of Clausen, who has been called college football's version of Lebron James, causing Irish fans to look beyond current starting quarterback and for-mer recruiting golden boy Brady Quinn. One can also enter into any number of message board discussions regarding Clausen, who allegedly showed up to his first collegiate press conference in a limousine, and other recruits. Clausen is seventeen years old.

"It's like anything else in that it can be good and bad," says Hagen, when I ask him about the impact of the Internet on college recruiting. It's an impact that, on a good day can simply be chalked up to overkill, but on a bad day can be described as downright creepy. It is a world of "inside sources" and forty-year-old men spending hours online debating the futures of seventeen-year-olds. But it speaks to our relentless desire for change, as the most popular kid in town is the kid who hasn't taken a snap yet. On recruiting Web sites, every kid is made to look and feel like the one who is going to lead good old State U to the Promised Land. But we forget that they are kids who have only had a driver's license for one year, and who have chemistry class troubles, girlfriend troubles, and troubles picking the campus where they may spend the next four years of their lives.

"You take what's said and written on those Web sites with a grain of salt," says Hagen of Rivals.com, Scout.com, and others like them. "You can get on and find out what a kid's numbers were at a combine or whatever. What's sad is that a lot of people pay money—fans and alumni—thinking those pages are 'the gospel' when it comes to recruiting.

"People think we get too many 'three-star' guys, and not enough four- or five-star guys," he continues. "I've got nothing against these guys who want to make a living but it's not the gospel truth. Sometimes a guy's best football is two or three years down the road. But those ratings are pretty arbitrary, based on a few clips of film. The key, for us, is to keep mistakes from a recruiting perspective at a minimum. The question is how many 'football players' without great measurables do we take? We can't take everybody like that. And how many 'athletes' do we take who maybe haven't shown it all on the field yet? You're banking on the fact that you can make them football players. We're looking at a lineman now who hasn't played much football, but he's 6-foot-7 and 265 and runs a 5.0, which is very fast for a lineman. You don't have the time you need in recruiting to get all of those questions answered. How is he going to respond when he starts getting smacked around? You can't have all of your guys fit that mold.

"I think recruiting's the most important thing we do, and it takes up so much of your time. That's the tough thing about college football. In the NFL they take every minute coaching the players. We don't have the luxury of going out in free agency and signing a guy to fill a void.

"I enjoy the people aspect of it. I do enjoy the travel, but at the same time it takes me away from my family. Getting to know the kids is great . . . early on it's a lot of phone conversations but getting into December and January there are more home visits."

I ask Hagen to describe those visits, as I have visions of him entering some pretty intimidating environments. I also wonder about an athletic culture where each kid is now his own franchise at a young age—wondering already about the NFL and what's in it for him.

"Sometimes it's no parents and there's a high school coach helping him make the decision. You need to find out what makes the guy tick. Are they a selfish person? Are they just looking out for themselves?

"Sometimes you go into a home and it's a single parent. But sometimes you get into a great family environment with two parents, who are very flattered and happy that you've taken the time out to come into their home. Other times it's clear that Mom and Dad are running the show and it's 'What can you do for my son?' Sometimes I'm in inner-city Chicago and sometimes I'm in suburban Indianapolis which is very affluent.

"I'll never forget my first day out as a college recruiter. When I was at Northern Illinois, Coach Novak sent me to Gary, Indiana, to visit with a couple of prospects. Gary is a tough town. I remember, rolling in there, realizing that I'd lived a very sheltered life. There's a great cultural divide at the 80/94 Highway in northern Indiana. North of the highway you have Gary and Hammond, which are both pretty rough areas, and to the South you have Valparaiso, Muenster, Merrilville, and areas that are more affluent.

It's an eye-opener, but it's also a privilege to go into people's homes and experience how they live."

There have been entire books written about the recruiting process—the most notable of which is *The Courting of Marcus Dupree* by the late Willie Morris. It chronicles in detail the days and weeks leading up to Dupree's decision to sign with the University of Oklahoma out of high school. It describes cloak-and-dagger exercises, complete with late-night meetings, car chases, and stakeouts—as Dupree was the Lebron James of his era. A man-child who many thought would change the game. But after a conflict with his college coach, Barry Switzer, he found himself, at nineteen, in the USFL and later, after a serious knee injury, out of football. A back-page blip in six-point font on the "Transactions" page. There are no sure things in the world of college recruiting.

The only sure thing, it seems, is that as long as there is recruiting, there will be schools that cheat. The most famous of such situations was the 1987 "death penalty" levied on the Southern Methodist University football program. According to a *Dallas Morning News* report in 1987:

> The Committee on Infractions report uncovered "stipulated" violations that thirteen football players were paid approximately $47,000 during the 1985–86 academic year and that eight student-athletes continued to receive payments from September to December 1986 of about $14,000.

The best college football programs are able to stay clean, or at least keep their indiscretions private. Some stay clean because they are, for the most part, clean. I wonder about the strain that the constant attention of older men puts on the average teenager during the recruiting process. Hagen tells the story of current starting DT Ryan Baker, who he calls "a dying breed."

"It was a process that played itself out into March or April, well after the national signing day," says Hagen, of a recruiting battle that pitted Purdue against Notre Dame for Baker's services. "He was truly conflicted. He wasn't in it to just get the attention, which a lot of people thought. People thought he was just eating up the recruiting and wanting to be on the front page. But from a leadership perspective he's just a quality guy. Not a selfish bone in his body. I wish there were more student athletes like that, but in this day and age it's more about instant gratification and 'What can you do for me now?' "

Football can be a great teacher of those lessons. Not everyone is going to be gratified in college football. I ask him about the day-to-day process with Baker and Notre Dame.

"I can remember we really felt like we needed a defensive tackle that could come in and play with us right away," he says. "I remember an hour-long phone conversation with Ryan when I was out in Los Angeles looking at another JUCO defensive lineman. It was very positive. I was selling him on why I thought he should come to Purdue. I got up the next morning, in California with the four-hour time difference, and turned on my phone to see that he had called late at night. When I called him back I was shocked to learn that he thought he was going to go to Notre Dame. They had used a tactic with him in recruiting where he felt like he needed to make a decision right away, or his scholarship was going to go to another player."

Coming out of Bishop Chatard High School, Baker was ranked as the nation's No. 3 tight end by Tom Lemming, as well as the No. 11 strongside defensive end and No. 2 player in Indiana by Rivals.com. He was a four-year starter at tight end and defensive end, and his list of accolades was lengthy: All-American, Indiana Gatorade Player of the Year, runner-up for Indiana Mr. Football, Indiana Defensive Lineman of the Year, Indianapolis Star City Player of the Year and team Most Valuable Player. As a senior he recorded 52 tackles, including 18 for loss and 8 sacks.

"He had gone to a Catholic high school and for him there was the idea that he had grown up dreaming about going to Notre Dame," says Hagen. "But I think, to be honest, he was just a second- or third-list guy for them.

"We talked later that day as I went back to the airport, and I sensed that he was conflicted, but at that point all I could do is wish him well. I thought a great deal of him as a kid, and his family. All you can do as a recruiter is say, 'Hey, if something changes here, give me a call.' The next day I was back in Chicago and got ahold of his parents to thank them for the opportunity to meet with their son. It's funny though, because we had already sent out the scholarship papers to his family—we send them out a few days before the signing date. I remember his dad calling me and saying 'What does this mean?' I told him it was just our policy and that he could tear them up. But at that point I just sensed that all was not right. That Friday I got a call from his mom and she was distraught, because he had lost ten or twelve pounds that week just worrying. I told her the door was still open for him to come to Purdue. That the option was still there, and that's really when the circus started.

"So the conversation started to pick up then. The poor kid was a mess. I remember the Tuesday night I got home and got a phone call about 10:30 . . . I was pretty wiped out after a trip and got a phone call from his dad. He wanted to know what time I'd be in the office the next day. Basically in a nutshell there were a lot of phone calls . . . he didn't sign with Notre Dame, and he didn't sign with us. It started about a six-week process where we just kept the scholarship open and kept communication. During that time period your patience is tested. You don't get into bashing another school; you just keep talking about the positives. I think about our patience throughout the process, which never waivered . . . we reissued papers several times. We were on spring break at the time when it ended. I was with my family in Florida and he called and said that he wanted to wait until basketball was over, but that he would sign with us.

"The poor kid got bashed back and forth. Everybody had an opinion on what he should do. My advice to him was just to get with your core—your mom, dad, and your family and lean on them. He knew he was a priority with us, but after signing day Notre Dame kind of backed off."

Baker has excelled for the Boilermakers. In 2005 he was named Academic All-Big Ten and appeared in all eleven games, including two starts. He had 10 tackles (7 solo, 3 assists), including 0.5 sacks and recorded a season-high 2 tackles (both solos) versus Notre Dame on October 1. In 2006, he has started nearly every game at defensive tackle.

Having gone through it, I remember the intensity of the relationships that are built through the recruiting process, but I also remember the stark changes that take place once a player arrives on campus as a freshman.

"As a coach you don't just turn off the relationship," says Hagen. "I coached him as a position coach for a year and a half, and he knew coming in that I always had an open door. Everything that I told him in the recruiting process held true. But he didn't want to just have a buddy-buddy kind of relationship. He wanted somebody to bust his tail to make him better. He's a dying breed, and very rare in that he wants to be great in everything he does. There are too many nowadays that think that because they're the star athlete, people are going to hand them a grade. That's why it's so refreshing to see people like Bake who want to earn everything.

"In fact, the other day he came in and told me he was getting a *C* in calculus, and he's used to getting nothing lower than a *B*. It was absolutely killing him."

CHAPTER 8

THE AGENT:
J. HARRISON HENDERSON III

IT'S BEEN A LONG DAY. Up at 3 A.M. for the hour-and-a-half drive to Detroit Metro, to catch the 6:30 A.M. to Pensacola. Then to the Hertz desk, where my $32.99 rental car soon turns into a $119 rental thanks to the magic of hidden fees, state charges, tire disbursement taxes, etc. Then an hour's drive to Mobile for a day's worth of Senior Bowl practices. By 9 P.M. I'm ready to crash, but sports agent Harrison (Harry) Henderson is just getting started.

We are winding our way through downtown Mobile, which in spots has a French Quarter flavor about it, in Henderson's SUV—filled to the brim with programs, scraps of paper, football preview magazines, and notebooks. It looks like a used bookstore on wheels, which is no knock, as I like used bookstores. I am experiencing that feeling I get when I meet older people (Harrison is in his early sixties) who have far more energy than I do. The feeling is shame.

We settle on an oyster bar, and in no time Henderson has produced a small, exotic-looking vial from his sport jacket, with Chinese writing on the label. The bar is bustling at 9:15 P.M., and its walls are lined with the various dignitaries and celebrities who have dined there. One must keep their head on a swivel at places like these, as you may find yourself talking about an NFL coach or player who ends up sitting just a booth or two away. However, I am having trouble keeping my eyes open at all.

"This stuff will make you strong," he says simply, convinced that the liquid in the vial contains the secret to strength and virility. I have been awake for nearly twenty hours. I catch his wrist just as he is about to pour the liquid into my glass of water.

"I'll be awake all night if I drink that stuff," I tell him, bleary-eyed. "Well, if you're interested in learning more, this stuff is un-believable" he says, before producing a business card. "It's all word of mouth. Unbelievable," he says again. Henderson, I learn, from Henderson, saved a man's life with this stuff. The guy had a broken back, or cancer, and this stuff saved his life. The guy was on twenty-five painkillers and after three months on the serum was pain-free, having sex again, and off antidepressants. I don't doubt him. Salesmen all have great stories, and they tell them convincingly. He gulps the mystery solution and then puts me through a battery of surreal tests of which I grab his wrists and he breaks the holds due, no doubt, to the high performance of the miracle liquid.

"Resist me, don't let me pull them apart," he says, as I strain against him. I am exhausted. "It's energy. Look it up. It's unbelievable. It helps change people's lives."

"I met a guy on the tennis court one day," he says, when I ask him how he came to be a sports agent. I will learn that Harrison often takes circuitous routes to his answers, but that those routes aren't always unpleasant. "We played and he beat me 6–2, 6–1, and I said, 'I'd like to play you again' and the next Saturday I beat him 6–0, 6–0. We became best friends, and he had worked for a guy named Steve Arnold who was definitely the first agent in football."

Arnold's first client was Bozo the Clown, of Chicago kid's television fame, but he ended up handling an endorsement deal for former Giants quarterback Y. A. Tittle. Tittle, as the story goes, was ready to do an endorsement for nothing—just happy to see his mug in a magazine. Arnold pursued a better deal for Tittle, who ended up making $1,000 on the deal. The rest, as they say, is history.

A well-traveled story about former Packers center Jim Ringo sheds some light on the history of the agenting businesses. In 1964 Ringo brought his financial advisor (agent) to help negotiate a contract with Vince Lombardi, the legendary, and fearsome, coach of the Green Bay Packers. Lombardi excused himself for a minute, when he returned he told the agent that he was negotiating with the wrong team. Ringo, it seems, had been traded to the Philadelphia Eagles in the time it had taken Lombardi to excuse himself. Though they have been around since the inception of the league, agents were few and far between before 1970. An operator named C. C. "Cash and Carry" Pyle is thought to be the first sports agent. The first account of negotiations came when Pyle negotiated a deal with the Chicago Bears for Red Grange to earn $3,000 per game and $300,000 in endorsement and movie rights. Grange is regarded by some as the pro game's first megastar, and the player who did the most to legitimize professional football—as it had theretofore been seen as subpar as compared to the college game.

Agents are defined as those individuals who secure employment and promotional deals for athletes; however, some now handle all aspects of an athlete's life and finances, from finding a home to preparing income taxes.

"Only the best players had agents in the early years," Henderson says. "My first client was a basketball player named Larry Drew, a point guard out of Missouri who was drafted by the Pistons in 1980." Drew had the misfortune of playing in the same backcourt with Isiah Thomas, who ended up becoming a pretty decent NBA point guard in his own right.

Henderson throws out names faster than my fatigued hands can write them. I momentarily regret not taking the Chinese miracle drops and consider asking for them. Besides the money, which I assume to be pretty good, I ask Henderson what he likes about the business.

"My mom was a scratch golfer," he says. "She would spot me a couple of strokes on the 5s, but would still beat me like a drum, so I took up tennis." Henderson was a college tennis player, ultracompetitive, and wanted to stay in sports. "My first passion in life is sports. I have tickets to everything."

There are still many in the league's old guard who would say that agents have contributed a great deal to ruining the game. I ask Harrison his opinions on the fairness of this stigma.

"If there were no agents," he says, "players would simply make a lot less money. They're the ones who could be maimed for life. A lot of them come out crippled. They're putting their bodies at risk and they're being paid to do it. It may still be a game, but it's also a business."

Having both played football and boxed, I think football is the most brutal thing I've ever done. Harrison sees himself as a protector of young athletes, someone who helps to shepherd the player into adulthood.

"We have ten clients this year," he says, of the upcoming draft class. The most notable of Henderson's clients is Justin Vincent, a big, fast tailback from LSU, who distinguished himself early in his college career, but then got lost in a crowded backfield with other standouts like Joseph Addai and Alley Broussard. "As a freshman

Justin got to play and at the SEC championship they beat Georgia and Justin was the MVP, and then he was the MVP of the national championship and was on the cover of *Sports Illustrated.*"

Vincent made his mark that first year, rushing for over 1,000 yards, but saw his carries and production dwindle in successive seasons.

"You know who I recruited that'll blow your mind?" Henderson asks, shifting gears. We will do this often during the meeting. The mention of one school or player will call to mind another school or player, attached to whom is a story.

"Who?"

"Anthony Carter. He selected me, but his wife who was on the city council and was six years older than he was, selected someone else." Carter finished his collegiate career as Michigan's all-time leader in receptions, and was a three-time All-American. He then went on to play thirteen seasons in the NFL and USFL, most notably with the Minnesota Vikings.

"Dominique Zeigler, WR, Baylor . . . thirteenth rated WR according to Mel Kiper," Henderson says, seamlessly shifting back to a discussion of his current draft clients. At press time Zeigler is currently fifth in school history in receptions with 112, and tied for ninth in touchdown grabs. He has size, at 6-foot-3 and 185, that makes scouts take notice, but toiled in relative obscurity at Baylor. "Another guy named Trent Shelton from Baylor who is ranked about the twenty-eighth receiver. Another RB Pierre Rembert, who used to be at Michigan, and was at Illinois State this year."

Rembert possesses ideal size at 6-foot and 220, but was lost in the shuffle at Michigan, where he had to compete with Mike Hart. He transferred to 1-AA Illinois State, where he led the Redbirds in rushing, but like Vincent faces an uphill battle for the attention of NFL scouts. Harrison gives a handful of other names, none of which I recognize. I ask Henderson how he finds these guys or rather, how they find him.

"Justin was a referral . . . I have tickets to the LSU games, and my family has had them for years," he says. "I had a player named Kevin Guidry in the 1988 draft. He was a real well-known, and well-respected guy. Real sharp guy. Kevin referred me to Justin."

I ask Henderson about his favorite clients over the years—guys that I would know—and he immediately mentions Ron Brown, the Arizona State receiver, perhaps best known for winning a gold medal on the U.S. 4x100 meter relay team in Los Angeles.

"Ronald came out of Arizona State where he played DB for three years," he says. "He only caught sixteen passes in his senior year, but ten were for touchdowns. Unbelievable speed. Ron was drafted in '83 in the second round by the Cleveland Browns. He didn't really like the cold weather, and he really wanted to be in a warm-weather place. They flew him in on draft day and left him in the airport for six hours. I negotiated a four-year contract for a million dollars, and $750,000 was guaranteed. We don't tell a player he has to take a deal, we just make recommendations. Ron turned it down. He didn't feel comfortable with it. And he didn't like the cold weather.

"So he came up with the idea that he would run in the Olympics," Harrison continues. "They've got one year to sign, and then they go back into the draft. He held out and didn't play the whole season. I supported him in the decision, but he's a football player and I felt like he needed to play football. We helped him some financially, but not a lot. Nothing like what they do now."

Now, a player is in the employ of the agent almost immediately after his last college game. He is bankrolled and flown to a world-class training facility that is somehow different from the world-class facility he is in at his Big Ten or SEC school. The player trains almost exclusively for events including the 40-yard dash, the three-cone drill, the bench press, and the vertical jump. "If you don't do training, you don't get the clients nowadays," he says. "I don't know who started it but that's the way it is."

So Ron Brown.

"What happened was, Steve Arnold and I got the Chargers involved, and they offered him $1.35 million, so it got serious, but after the trade deadline it was all over," he says. "We started getting interest after the season because Ron was so fast. He ran a 4.25 in the 40-yard dash. In '83 and '84 he beat Carl Lewis twice. We had to get permission from the NFLPA to seek a trade for him. Then the 49ers got interested and offered $1.75 million for four years of football. Finally the Rams offered $2.25 for four years of football. It was a two-year no-trade."

All of this for a player who managed just under 1,800 yards and 13 scores—for his career. It is an example of how big this business is, for relatively oblivious kids. Now, he says, the competition includes financial advisors.

"They're as competitive as the agents," he says.

Harrison is a realist, however, when it comes to impacting a kid's draft position.

"There's nothing I can do physically to help a guy," he says. "In ways I can, if I can talk to a guy, keep him out of trouble, and keep him focused. But it's all debatable. All of these trainers are saying they're better than the other guy.

"Don't get me wrong, I think the agent is important. I think a player can screw up by picking the wrong agent. It's competitive. It's a very tough business. When you're driven by money, people will do anything. It's really kind of sad. Where there's big money, there's big problems."

But is it as shady as it's perceived?

"There was an agent in the eighties who was very successful, but he's working somewhere as a cook now," Henderson says, cryptically. "He thought the rules didn't apply to him.

"When you're honest, and you follow the rules and regulations, you still get bad-mouthed by the unethical guys," he says.

"I also represented Sam Graddy who played for the Broncos and Raiders and was in the Olympics," he says. Graddy wasn't initially sure he wanted to play professional football. But in those days many teams, especially Kansas City, Denver, Seattle, and Dallas would all bring 150 guys to camp. Most teams brought over 100. So fringe players like Graddy with tools, but not production, had a chance to show if they had what it took to succeed on the NFL level. According to Henderson, Graddy "only caught about ten balls" at Tennessee.

"He played a couple of years in Denver and every pass he caught was for about 45 yards," he says, embellishing the numbers as only an agent can. Graddy's official statistical resume shows one catch for 30 yards, in two seasons as a Denver Bronco. "Then he spent about five years with the Raiders. I knew the Raiders liked track guys so I got in touch with Al Davis.

"Sam was winning the 100 meters against Carl Lewis in the 1984 Olympics," he says. "He was a nineteen-year-old freshman at Tennessee at the time. He looked back over his shoulder to see where Carl Lewis was, and it cost him the gold medal. Don't ever look back. He could have been a household name.

"This tends to be sort of a burn-out business," he says. "It's high-pressure and high intensity. You've gotta be ready to answer the player's call whenever they need help, 24-7."

I ask Henderson if he does a lot of, for lack of a better term, hand-holding with his clients.

"Well, I have a young guy, Lucas Chizzonite, who works for me, and he does a lot of the stuff like taking them to workouts, taking them out to eat, and the stuff later at night," he says. "I'll go eat with them and do a little of that but I'm more of a guy who goes to bed a little earlier.

"I tell people I don't always represent the best players, but if I represent them they're good people," he says.

"Eric Moulds is the big player I represent now," he says. "Eric has earned probably $18 million in signing bonuses. I saw him here in the Senior Bowl and I knew he would be good. And he's a great person. He's a down-to-earth guy from Mississippi, but he had challenges along the way. It was beneficial that he had someone like me. It's been a real joy to be involved with people like that."

Though he loves college football, Henderson still gets annoyed at what he perceives to be a "holier than thou" attitude toward his profession.

"The college people don't want the agents coming in," he says, "but the shit they do . . . oh, boy. These guys grow up being worshipped and put on a pedestal, but it can sort of lead to a 'not being in the real world' outlook.

"But there are a lot of really good kids," he says back in the SUV, shifting back into sales mode. "Justin Vincent, for example, a great kid."

CHAPTER 9

THE NFL DRAFT GURU:
TODD MCSHAY, ESPN

TODD MCSHAY IS a little sick of talking about the NFL Draft. Not on work time, but at parties and normal social gatherings. It is his job to think about, watch, talk about, and meditate on every draft-worthy college player, every year for the foreseeable future. It is a job he loves, just not in social situations.

"I get sick of football in a social environment," he says. "When you go to visit friends or go to a party and it's all people want to talk about. You'd rather, for once, spend time talking about something else."

I catch up with McShay in Mobile, Alabama, at the Senior Bowl, and for the most part he blends with the rest of the early-thirty-something football-nut crowd that has assembled there. It is a trip he has made for the last ten years, beginning in 1996 when he was still in college, covering the Senior Bowl for free. He now covers the event as a paid staff member at ESPN, which you recognize as the company most responsible for your soaring cable bills and lack of productivity at work. McShay, just a shade under thirty, is the real deal now.

"I went to the University of Richmond, which is a 1-AA school to play football and wound up injuring my back in my second year," he says. "I was a walk-on and didn't have much of a future as a player. So I talked to the coaches and was able to stay on as a student assistant coach. At the same time, through my grandfather who was a recruiting guy at the University of Michigan, I was able to get an internship with a guy named Gary Horton." He spells Horton's name for me.

"Horton had just left the NFL, after working for Belichick with the Browns, and in Tampa Bay. He was basically starting up an independent scouting company that would act as a cross-check for NFL clubs as well as generating content for the public. His vision was to do all of that, and to align it as the 'thirty-third personnel department.' He and I hit it off and he had me doing work while I was still in school. I lived on his couch for nine months in New York. It was nothing glamorous. You think about a thousand bucks a month in Midtown and you get the idea. Then the *Sporting News* came into the picture."

I ask McShay if that was a "cha-ching" moment or a "good, now we can eat" sort of moment for the fledgling company.

"It was 'good, now we can eat,' " he says quickly. "There was more room for content and in-depth content. Even when I worked with Gary over the summer and when I first got in I focused the most on the draft stuff. It's always been my drive and the biggest focus."

The initial company, called The War Room, included McShay, Horton, Dean Dalton, Jim Nagy, and Jeremy Green who is Dennis

Green's son. McShay took over when Green left briefly to be a scout for the San Francisco 49ers. Green has returned to what is now called Scouts, Inc.

"We went from War Room to Scouts, Inc.," he says. "ESPN decided to buy us out and we got out of the NFL business. As of now I'm an ESPN employee. It's been good for me because they have so many outlets and have allowed me to expand what they do."

At its apex as an independent company, they served as many as sixteen NFL clubs in some capacity.

"We worked as a cross-check, just as one more opinion," he says. "If they viewed a guy as a first-rounder, and I came in and evaluated him as a fourth-rounder, they would at least take a look at that guy again. It really legitimized us to the *Sporting News* and ESPN. The logic was 'if it's good enough to be on Jon Gruden's desk it's good enough to be on yours.'

"I can remember the third or fourth draft in, having teams call during the draft and saying 'we've got these three guys on the board, what do you think?' I'm just very fortunate that it all fell together, we were at the right place at the right time."

McShay's process for a given draft happens in May, two weeks after the previous draft. He puts together a "board" containing all of the players he feels he needs to be watching starting in March, at college pro-days. He watches ten hours of film a day, nonstop, in May and June.

"I take July off and then during the season we break it up by position weekly," he says. "If I wrote twenty quarterbacks up during the spring, I'll write up any guys that I missed during the spring. I'll then evaluate the All-Star film, practices, the combine, and then write the final report."

McShay is pulled in a number of directions during the pre-draft period, doing radio and television appearances almost every day. It is a tightrope, he says, between disseminating as much information as possible, and protecting the quality of that information by having enough time left to do the homework.

"You can only give away so many hours," he says, "because you need the information to be up to quality."

The topic of Mel Kiper, the world's foremost draft guru, is broached. I wonder if they interact, and if Kiper sees McShay as a threat or vice versa.

"I interact with him regularly professionally," he says. "We interact on radio shows, and in this year's draft guide we did a Kiper versus McShay kind of thing. I talk to him socially once in a while. Early on, he was the guy I was chasing because I didn't know him. Now I've gotten to know him well enough and he's been so supportive of me that it's not at all a competition. I wanted so badly to prove that my stuff is better than Mel Kiper's but that's not what it's like anymore."

A Google search for "NFL Draft" reveals no less than 2,540,000 hits on the subject, and ESPN's telecast of the event has become a TV draw of almost Super Bowl–ian proportions. Nationally, the first day of the 2006 draft had a rating of 4.7, or 4.22 million households, helping make it the highest-rated draft in ESPN's twenty-seven-year history of broadcasting the event. And because of the wild subjectivity of the content, every fan, regardless of experience, feels a certain ownership of his team and that team's picks.

"If you talk to the Cleveland Browns about one player, and the Houston Texans about another player, they could have completely opposite opinions," he says.

"My parents both work for Delta Airlines," he says. "My dad took the retirement and my mother is wishing she did too."

I ask McShay what his parents think of his occupation as a draftnik.

"My dad isn't much of a sports fan, but he's excited for me because I'm doing what I love to do," he says. "But my mother is fanatical. It was her dad who worked at the University of Michigan and I would go to Michigan games constantly. I knew Bo Schembechler, Lloyd Carr when he was an assistant, Les Miles and all those guys. It really helped me being around the game. She's thrilled. Forget it. Every single day she talks to me about it."

I ask McShay if he is at a spot, professionally, where he has begun to be recognized as a "personality."

"Yeah, within the last year more so," he says. "At the draft and maybe here, where people are so tuned into the draft stuff. Every once in a while at airports, which my wife hates. She doesn't hate it she just does her best to ground me."

McShay also does ESPN Radio College GameDay with Dave Revsine and Gerry DiNardo for seven hours each Saturday and that exposure, he says, has contributed a great deal to his public recognition.

"Just hearing the name all the time," he says.

Though there is subjectivity, a draft pundit is only as good as his outcomes, so I ask McShay if there are players that perhaps he championed, who have gone on to successful careers.

"I was on Tom Brady," he says. "I wouldn't have, by any means, said he would have been a first-round pick. But we always sold the fact that he was the most underrated player in that draft. He got a raw deal because of Henson and all of the hype he got."

Upon his arrival at Michigan, Brady was seventh on the depth chart and had an uphill battle for playing time that was so intense that he hired a sports psychologist to help him cope with frustration and anxiety and even considered transferring. Brady split time with Michigan prep phenom and golden boy Drew Henson, but ended up starting every game in the 1998 and 1999 seasons. In his first full year as starter, he set Michigan's record for most completions in a season (214). He was All-Big Ten both seasons and team captain his senior year. The Wolverines won twenty of twenty-five games when Brady started and shared the Big Ten

Conference title in 1998. Brady capped that season off with a win over Arkansas in the Citrus Bowl. In the 1999 season, Brady led Michigan to an overtime win in the Orange Bowl over Alabama, throwing for 369 yards and four touchdowns. Brady was selected by the New England Patriots with the 199th pick of the 2000 NFL Draft—a pick that the Patriots almost used on Louisiana Tech quarterback Tim Rattay.

"It's hard to think back because once they're drafted a guy can go into the league and get into the right system. There are so many variables.

"I honestly never thought LaDainian Tomlinson would be this good," he says of the All-Pro San Diego running back. "I remember watching him on film at TCU and they ran the option. A lot of his yards he got moving upfield, on the pitch, in the crease. But I was younger then, and every year that goes by I learn ten more things . . . a new trend. I should have focused more on the fact that Tomlinson caught the ball well, and blocked well. I should have focused more on special teams."

The players who do end up making it—navigating their way out of a hometown, into college, and then into the murky world of money and success in the NFL keeping their noses clean in the process—prove to be incredible survivors. The name Charles Rogers is mentioned.

"You talk about missing on a guy," McShay says, "I thought he was going to be great."

There is danger in taking a wide receiver in the first round, and the Lions, with high-priced failures like Rogers and Mike Williams, are exhibit A. The winner of the 2002 Biletnikoff Award, Rogers still holds school records for most TDs in a career with 27, breaking the record held by former Spartans WR (and later MLB icon) Kirk Gibson and the school record for most receiving yards in a single game with 270. He was drafted second overall in the 2003 NFL Draft by the Detroit Lions, one selection ahead of two-time Pro Bowl WR Andre Johnson. For whatever reason, the first-round receiver seems to be a prime candidate for the NFL flake-out.

"It's like a chip gets imbedded in their brain," he says. Our discussion of receivers leads into a discussion of the game itself, and how the culture has changed so much in just the last ten years.

"I was listening to Mike and Mike the other morning—those guys are crazy—and they were talking about, I think it was [Seahawks WR] Deion Branch in the first playoff game they had, he caught an 8-yard in route and then just got up and freaked out," he says. "The culture has completely changed. It's me, me, me."

The character piece of the projection is equally as huge as the physical production. There are twenty-one-year-olds who are as mature and capable mentally as they are physically, and there are others who have no business being professionals at anything, much less making seven-figures in the NFL.

"The Patriots are a great example," he says. "They 'got it' before everyone else got it. You don't have to be the nicest guy or the best guy but you have to buy in."

I ask McShay how long he sees himself in the draft guru business—watching film, taking the trips to Mobile and Indianapolis each year to chase twenty-one-year-olds. He answers, unwaveringly, that this is his thing.

"I've had offers to take personnel jobs in the league," he says. "I came so close. In 2003 I was within two hours of taking a job with the Browns, and it would have been a nightmare because the whole staff got fired the next year. I've had offers to go into the in-house scouting departments of several teams."

I would think, as a former athlete, the chance to be a part of a team again would be incredibly tempting.

"The ultimate competition, for me, is being a part of a personnel department that puts it all together," he says. "But the more I'm around it and the more I talk to people in the league, the more

I think the pipe dream may not be worth it. There's a lot of insta-bility, pressure, and competitiveness. Scouts are on the road all the time. They don't have any decision-making power either. A lot of guys are just private investigators—the GMs say 'go get the height, weight, and speed and then we'll make a decision about the guy.' Everyone who comes out of scouting, in the league, seems very hardened by it. Lots of gossiping."

McShay takes several calls through the course of the interview, at least one from his wife. He has been in Mobile for the entire week, staying in a hotel out of the city, near the airport. He has to tape a radio interview yet tonight, as well as type up some reports. I thank him for the pleasure of interviewing a good communica-tor, after speaking largely with athletes for the past forty-eight hours. He asks me my best interview thus far.

"Brian Leonard's parents," I tell him, before asking him, on the way out, where he sees Leonard going on Draft Day.

CHAPTER 10

THE WALK-ON:
MAX POLLOCK, LB, UNIVERSITY OF MICHIGAN

IT'S NOT CHARM, so much as it is spectacle. It's hard to feel charmed by a place where you have to pay fifteen bucks to park. But you get caught up in the grandeur of the Big House. Of being one of a throng of 100,000 in Michigan Stadium. The rows and rows of gleaming sport-utility vehicles parked on the same fairways where their drivers play golf during the summer. The tailgates sporting gourmet chefs instead of hot dogs and Miller Lites. The sun is shining and everyone is prospering—their degrees having paid off.

"I think I'm the only Michigan graduate not making six figures," says Regner, my buddy and a currently unemployed UM

Film Studies grad, as he maneuvers his own heavily used SUV through campus. "I want to park at my old house," he says, creeping down the street as we look at row upon row of houses with ambitious maize-shirted frat boy types collecting dollars for parking in one hand and guzzling cheap beer from the other. These are the selfsame guys that will be handling your mutual funds and trying to sleep with your daughter in a few years.

The game is against Central Michigan, an early-season contest boasting little in the way of a challenge, but the game is secondary to the spectacle at this point. Michigan will pound Central today, but will they do it to the satisfaction of their nation of supporters—ranging from rich alums to the guy who lives down the street and just likes the helmets.

Regner wheels the Jeep Cherokee into the driveway of the house he thinks was his. The underage-looking guy with the Natty Light can in his hand directs us to a space between two trees, and Regner deftly maneuvers the vehicle into the spot. He is an eternal pessimist, and every year braces himself for a disappointing season—that way, if it happens he is ready, or so the logic goes. He has convinced himself that quarterback Chad Henne cannot throw, and wide receiver Steve Breaston cannot catch. Despite the shining sun, the glorious surroundings, and the band-sounds of college football, he is miserable.

"I don't think this was my place," he says, walking backwards while looking up at the house and its boozy inhabitants. "Our place had an old tree in the front yard. But at least we won't need our rain jackets."

We make a long walk through the throng of tailgating fans, lined up in neat rows along the fairways and greens of a golf course adjacent to the stadium. The tailgate is almost serene compared to some I have seen, which are just a beer or two away from chaos. Even the music is laid back—somebody is playing a "Best of Lionel Richie" album, which, of course, draws snickers and rolled eyes from our group. Finally, a group of Wolverine women's volleyball players, clad in their game uniforms, approaches us to hand out flyers for that afternoon's game, beginning at the conclusion of the football game. The women have an almost radiant glow—I think most current supermodels were probably once college volleyball players. They encourage us to come to their game.

"I would show up to watch those girls do algebra," says our buddy AJ, wide-eyed, as they walk away.

The game is much as one might expect when a Big Ten power squares off with a Mid American Conference opponent—there is little in the way of drama. The bulk of the entertainment involves the band appearing, the drum major doing the drum major thing, and finally the team bursting out of a side tunnel and jumping up to touch the maize and blue banner present at every home game. As an eighty-year-old man, something about this will probably take my breath away. At least I hope so.

I engage in a spirited discussion with another fan in our section—she is the quintessential Ann Arbor six-figure hippie—about my first book, *Facing Tyson*. I occasionally take a reprieve from the conversation about my favorite author (sarcasm), to look down at the action on the field.

Perhaps the most notable event during the game is the appearance of a nasty thunderstorm that calls a halt to the game and, for the first time in stadium history, sends the players indoors for the better part of two hours. From the upper rim of the stadium we had a perfect vantage point to watch a black cloud roll ominously toward us, until it finally burst open, directly over the large bowl. The PA asks fans to vacate the stadium and go to their cars until further instruction, though a mass of humanity forms in the open-air concourse and we all get soaked by a cold rain. I am trapped next to a short woman who looks up at me and comfortingly explains that at least she won't be struck by lightning.

Eventually the players return and, like a baseball game, we are engaged in conversation almost the entire time, on topics such as the fact that the Wolverines have a freshman tailback named "Mister" Simpson; and whether or not it is appropriate for a grown man to wear the replica jersey of his favorite college star. We agree that there is something a little bit creepy about this, as there is an abundance of forty-year-old men in Chad Henne jerseys stalking the bowl.

The stands have begun to clear a bit early in the fourth quarter, as head coach Lloyd Carr is giving the bulk of the playing time to backups and younger players. A linebacker enters the game for the Wolverines wearing No. 51. I take note of this because he is small and white, and I was once the small, white linebacker, many years ago. I watch his movements closely, and read in the program that he is a senior walk-on with a decorated academic record who has played very little in his four-year career.

The Wolverines begin the series with Central backed up in their own end zone, the South end zone, where we have moved down and occupied the seats left by an old alum who has undoubtedly left to get a jump on the traffic. Here, down lower, one can hear the sounds of the game more acutely—the crack of plastic on plastic, the whistles, etc. Max Pollock lines up at left outside linebacker, and the Chippewas immediately split multiple wide receivers to his side, meaning that he will be forced to cover a player who is no doubt faster than he is. I get a little worried for him. At the snap, Pollock takes his drop, keeping his eyes fixed in the backfield on quarterback Dan LeFevour, as he scans the field. LeFevour then lofts the football in Pollock's direction. "Wow, he might get to make a play," I think to myself, as he plucks the errant pass out of the sky and begins to rumble, shocked no doubt, toward the South end zone where he is mobbed immediately by his teammates. The fans in my section shout their approval.

Max Pollock's mother, from Takoma Park, Maryland, has a bit of an East Coast–meets–Great Britain tinge in her voice. When she says "hello" on the telephone I imagine her sitting in some dark, wood-paneled room having a spot of brandy, in front of a crackling fire. She passes along his number and we agree to meet for coffee in Ann Arbor.

Pollock is a 218-pound walk-on linebacker, enrolled in the College of Literature and Arts. He looks like a real person—albeit athletic—in an age when college linebackers typically look like chemistry experiments gone awry. Blame it on the supplements. He is a fourth-year senior, and has appeared in exactly six games in his career. His most notable achievements are the UM-Athletic Academic Achievement awards that appear next to his name in the media guide.

We meet at a Starbucks in Ann Arbor, a town that in many ways is one giant Starbucks—it has retained an earthy, liberal sensibility despite the fact that most of the hippies there are well-off and drive gigantic SUVs. Students sit, plugged into iPods, throughout the coffee shop, studying and doing what normal students do. There are a lot of North Face jackets and fashionably torn jeans in the room. Ann Arbor's young people look much like those that you might find in Telluride or Aspen. There is a healthy, prosperous, outdoorsy glow about them.

"I kind of regret not having this experience," Pollock says, after we sit down. "You know, kids going to Starbucks and studying, and having all-night study sessions and stuff—doing their college thing. I guess I was never really afforded that option with football, when you have practice every morning. It is like a full-time job, but I maybe missed out on the college lifestyle. I try to reach out to new things but it's definitely hard when you have an every-day commitment."

He has come straight from a four-hour practice this morning, this coming after a three-hour affair last night in preparation for the Wolverines' bowl trip to Pasadena. He is dressed like the other students—baggy "Michigan" sweatshirt, jeans, and a Washington Nationals ballcap. There is nothing about him that screams Football Player. And, indeed, nobody seems to notice our presence.

"For me, nobody would be able to look at me and say, 'he's a football player,' " he says. "But my closest friends on the team all happen to be these massive brutes. When I'm with them people tend to look at me as a football player, or at least a hanger-on. But it's cool, when people value the football team as much as they do at the University of Michigan, it's definitely cool to be able to tell people that I play. Especially when they might not assume that I do, because of the fact that I take real classes and get good grades. People often assume that you're dumb because you play football. It's not like you have to be some dumb jock because you play. That's been my favorite part of the whole thing."

As it turns out, my gut feeling about his parents was correct—his mother did postgraduate work at Harvard, and his father has both graduate and postgraduate degrees from Harvard. His mother owns a graphic-design firm and his father works for the United States State Department and is currently deployed in Iraq, though he was in the Big House for "the interception." Neither, oddly, had any athletic background.

"My parents don't have an athletic bone in their bodies," he says. "I mean, my dad plays tennis and runs once in a while, and my mom was more inclined towards the arts."

Pollock didn't begin organized football until his sophomore year of high school when a friend on the team encouraged him to join the squad. He went on to be voted the most accomplished athlete at Takoma Park High School in Maryland, but hadn't planned on playing college football.

"My first day of practice as a sophomore, the first day I'd ever put on pads, they made me captain of the jayvee team, though I'm not sure why," he recalls with honesty. He goes on to explain that after his high school career, and a breakup with a girlfriend, he didn't have any desire to continue his football career in college.

"I thought I'd hung up the cleats and would just go to college," he says. "I was mostly being recruited by Ivy League schools but I didn't want to go there . . . I have this idea, and maybe it's a misconception, that the Ivy Leagues are snobby or snooty."

I agree with this misconception.

"I have family in Ann Arbor—my uncle is a prof at U of M and my aunt lives here as well. The way that walking on came about is that my aunt, who's very outgoing and gregarious, asked me if I had ever thought about playing football in college. We happened to be walking through campus past the football building at the time and she said, 'Let's go in here and see what they have to say.' So we walk in and my aunt—being the outgoing person she is—said that we needed to see Coach Carr about her nephew walking on to the team. I remember sitting up there in my chair, with my head back, trying to look big and make my neck swell a little bit. When I was sitting in Schembechler Hall I was approached by an older man who said, 'Hello, young man,' and shook my hand. When he left, my aunt kind of nudged me and I saw him walking into an office with the name BO SCHEMBECHLER on the door. I felt like a complete idiot. I mean this guy was the epitome of Michigan Football."

Pollock then sent game film to the coaching staff, and waited to hear from them as to his future.

"To this day we have the call saved on our answering machine at home," he says. "It was coach Bill Sheridan, kind of in tough Midwestern coach voice, he said, 'We have a spot for you on the 115 and we expect you to report the first day of classes.' From that point on I guess I was a part of the team."

Pollock went on to describe a harrowing first several days in camp. The name on his locker was misspelled, and the freshman walk-on basically kept to himself.

"It's not that the older guys are mean to you," he says, "they just keep to themselves and really don't acknowledge you. But I was in a locker room with the freshmen and eventually those guys—Jake Long, Adam Kraus, Will Paul, Pat Sherril, and Garret Rivas—became my best friends. That was our little group. It's good to have those things as a freshman because otherwise you just kind of wander aimlessly around the building."

Pollock's first practices saw him playing defensive end, against the country's finest college players—many of whom were on their way to the NFL.

"I would alternate reps with a few of the other guys," he remembers. "I would inevitably mess everything up. Even the simplest looks I was supposed to be giving the offense I would screw up. The line was a pretty veteran line and they would all yell at me jokingly. And the coaches would always yell at me, like 'Who are you, some walk-on freshman?'

"I knew who some of the guys were because I followed Michigan football—I knew who Chris Perry and John Navarre were—but I never talked to them."

I ask Pollock if he sometimes marvels at the skills of the athletes he finds himself squaring off against in practice. He says that the best football player he has ever seen is Jason Avant, now a wide receiver with the Philadelphia Eagles. Avant, he says, did everything right on the practice field as well as on game days.

"It became a joke with a lot of the guys," he says. "Jason would make a play and we would all say, 'there goes the best football player I've ever seen.' "

Pollock, like most college seniors, is preoccupied with the decision about what to do "next year."

"The NCAA has a rule that if you have been on scholarship at any time in your career, and have been taken off, then you can't go back on again," he explains. Pollock was briefly on scholarship last year after the fifth-year seniors left the program in the spring. "But then they signed the new recruits and it ate up all the scholarships. It's part of the decision-making process, and I'd like to take some heat off my parents. I mean, I'm not going to play in the NFL, but there's nothing like this [football], and I've been told by the older guys that if I stop now I'll regret it. I won't ever be able to hit anybody again.

"Now I take it for granted . . . every rep in practice. It's been hard deciding to come back. Most of my friends have a probable career in the NFL. I'm deciding whether to go to law school or teach or something and they're deciding whether to jump to the NFL and make millions of dollars."

Pollock's degree will be in American Culture, which is interdisciplinary, he tells me. It is the first time I have ever heard the word "interdisciplinary" in an athlete interview.

"I was approached yesterday by a recruiter from Teach for America," he says. "They said that all I have to do is apply and they'll have a spot for me. I always thought about teaching, but truthfully with football I haven't given a lot of thought to what I want to do."

I feel for Pollock. Deciding what one wants to be when he grows up is a feeling that never goes away. Neither does wanting to put on a football helmet one more time. I begin to tell him about the project, and how I was in the stands that day when he scored against Central Michigan. I knew I wanted to interview him when I heard him use the word "surreal" later that week on the *Lloyd Carr Show*.

"The coach told me before the game that there was a pretty good chance that I would play," he says. "I've been fortunate this year to work some with the second-team, backing up different guys at different positions. I never thought it would turn out like it did. I thought I'd get the last few snaps in the game. I got in almost at the beginning of the fourth quarter. That was pretty amazing for me. That was the best thing for me, being in a game that wasn't already completely over. The first play I was in I got pancaked and my coach gave me a hard time about that. I can't blame it on nervousness, because he probably just got the best of me. But the only way to get comfortable in football is to hit somebody hard on the first play or get hit hard. And the next play was the interception.

"You almost don't believe that it happened. For instance, when I'll be watching ESPN and they're talking about the Michigan defense creating turnovers I'll think to myself, 'Hey, I did that once.' It definitely makes you feel more a part of the team.

"It's hard as a walk-on who might not make the travel team, while they're off doing their thing it's hard when it gets to game time. It's two different worlds. The interception made me feel like, hey, I'm on the stat-sheet, I'm in the record books."

Pollock recalls his other playing experiences, mostly on the last series of games that were well in hand. This is sometimes known as "mop-up duty" or "junk-time." His first game reps came in his sophomore year, in a blowout over Northwestern.

"We were up by a pretty big lead, and my coach put me in and just told me to play linebacker," he says. "I didn't know which spot to play, but I made the last tackle of the game and that was kind of my claim to fame up until the interception."

The game immediately following the Central Michigan game this season saw the Wolverines travel to Notre Dame, where they blew out the Irish under the gaze of Touchdown Jesus. Pollock was able to play on the same field where another walk-on, Rudy Ruettiger, had his one shining moment decades before.

"After the Notre Dame game when my friends and family saw me get in, they were even more excited for me than the interception," he says. "It doesn't get much better than playing at Notre Dame. Well, Michigan Stadium is better, but Notre Dame is a close second."

His parents have since become rabid college football fans—reading every magazine and Web site available on the sport.

"My mom probably knows more about college football right now than I do," he says. "I don't know how they're going to be when I finally stop playing but I think they're pretty hooked on it."

I ask Pollock if, early on, in the midst of so many practices without playing time, there were ever times that he entertained quitting.

"They're never going to make it easy on you, since you're a walk-on," he says. "With that, every day you're competing against guys who were All-Americans and five-star recruits. It can be discouraging. There were times when I thought ,'Maybe this isn't for me.' But at the end of the day you say I am a part of the Michigan football team. I'm part of a tradition that's gone on for hundreds of years."

Life, for the walk-on, is not made any easier by the NCAA who only allows the scholarship athletes such privileges as eating in the football complex training table each day.

"The big thing, through my experiences as a walk-on, is with the scholarship rules mandated by the NCAA, the whole team practices together but only the eighty-five scholarship players can go to the training table," he says. "Coach Carr makes the point of saying if he had it his way—and I believe he's sincere—that everybody would go to the training table, but it's all tied up in NCAA bureaucracy."

Regarding fame, I ask Pollock if he is on the EA Sports NCAA Football game, which is sort of the litmus test for college football players. Somewhat ashamedly, I admit that I still play these games.

"There's a linebacker on the game with my jersey number," he says, with a pause, "but the guy is black." He pauses a bit on the word because, in football circles it is still fine to say "black" but in ultra-enlightened Ann Arbor, it may well be verboten. "I think it's supposed to be one of our freshman, but there's nobody else on the team that wears No. 51. But Garrett Rivas created me on his game, which was a nice move by him."

Pollock waves hello to a female classmate, and we both glance at a table full of coeds, hard at word writing algebraic equations on note cards.

"When I see students out walking around I sometimes wonder what they do with the rest of their day," he says. "But I guess I'll find out in a year or two. I'll probably be bored out of my mind without a football practice to go to. Although you'll never hear me say that now because sometimes practice is the last thing I want to do. But I can't imagine life without it. It's such a huge part of my life in college. I can't even fathom that."

At some level there is a breath of fresh air, to experience college without football. You meet real friends, who don't play football, but you also miss it and feel lost without the regimentation. Pollock explains how important it is, to him, to have friends outside of the game, and explains that he has never lived with football players. I begin to pack up my notebook and tape recorder, but remember to ask him, finally, how it feels to run out of the tunnel in front of 100,000 plus and slap the Maize banner, as is tradition at each UM home game.

"That's a tradition I didn't know too much about before I got here," he says. "The way it works is that we go out to warm up before the game and the stadium may only have 25,000 people in it because it is a while before game time. Then you go back to the locker room for a while. It's completely awe-inspiring when you go back out to the tunnel and see the seats that were empty are completely filled. One hundred ten thousand people there to watch you. Coach always tells us that every time we run out of that tunnel is one closer to being our last."

CHAPTER 11

THE MOST BIZARRE RECRUITMENT IN RECENT HISTORY:

RONALD JOHNSON AND THE UNIVERSITY OF SOUTHERN CALIFORNIA

IF RONALD JOHNSON tears ligaments in his ankle, blows a knee, or, God forbid, runs into trouble with the law somewhere along the way, none of what I'm about to write will make any difference. But right now Ronald Johnson is a 6-foot, 177-pound WR/DB widely regarded as the best of such high school players in the nation. He is what is called a "five-star" recruit for those taken with assigning star values to teenagers from our nation's urban areas.

Johnson, his family, his friends, his high school coach Tony Annese, and a handful of members of the media have literally risked life and limb by driving through a snowstorm to assemble at a small Muskegon church for what amounts to a Ronald Johnson tribute program that will also include his college announcement. There will be speeches by Annese, a grandmother, his mother, his father, a newspaper reporter, a judge, and finally Ronald Johnson (who from this point forward will be called Rojo), who has prominently displayed T-shirts from some of his top college choices including Florida, Michigan State, Michigan, Ohio State, and USC. He will, it has been rumored, eliminate the schools that have spent tens of thousands of dollars recruiting him, by holding up and then tossing aside the T-shirts.

I will not be attending the ceremony and will use as my excuse the weather, which is indeed really terrible. However, deep down, I have trouble with all of this—with these ceremonies that have become painfully cliche, with the athlete using T-shirts or ballcaps to build drama surrounding a decision that has been debated into the ground by middle-age Internet pundits for months. Something about it doesn't feel right, so I will watch a video feed of the event, which also doesn't feel right, but feels less not right.

As is often the case with high school athletes of his stature, Rojo looks like a man among boys on his high school highlight videos. These videos all take on a certain similarity—the grainy, wobbly presentation, and the ordinary high school kids left in the wake of the phenom on various scoring plays including long passes, kickoff returns, interceptions for touchdowns, etc. Usually the videos are set to rap music but not always. But they all leave you with the same feeling: This kid is a tremendous athlete and he needs to go to My School.

As the Rojo tracking hit its apex in late January, it was understood that he would be going to the University of Michigan to play for Lloyd Carr and noted recruiter Ron English, the Wolverines' defensive coordinator. According to Rivals.com, Rojo runs the 40-yard dash in 4.48 seconds, and bench presses 280 pounds. He also, according to Rivals, has a twenty-eight-inch vertical jump.

Fairly early in the recruiting process, Michigan State offered a scholarship to Rojo's younger brother Corey Johnson, or, Cojo as a pre-emptive measure intended to lure Rojo into the fold. The gesture was widely regarded as for naught, however, as Rojo seemed solidly headed for the University of Michigan. This is where rumors begin to take over, and fact takes a backseat to hundreds of message boards where recruiting and the future of seventeen-year-olds are discussed twenty-four hours per day.

Despite my best intentions, I stayed abreast of the Rojo rumors via a couple of buddies who are rabid UM fans, and with whom I have lunch every couple of weeks.

"What's the latest on Rojo?" was my usual opening question, followed by responses like, "Ron English was the only one who was with him through the knee injury, so he's going to Michigan." Or, "A reliable source tells me that the entire Florida staff flew up on a private jet this weekend to meet with Rojo and his mother. It's Florida." Or, "His mom is mad at Michigan so it's either Florida or USC . . . or it might be Michigan State."

As I type this, roughly twenty-four hours before National Signing Day, February 7, 2007, it's difficult to walk past a group of youngish men anywhere in Michigan's lower peninsula without overhearing a Rojo conversation. Michigan State's fan base has convinced itself that landing Rojo would be Step 1 in the program's comprehensive rebuilding effort, this for a program that seems to have been rebuilding since the late 1980s. The University of Michigan fan, meanwhile, assumes that Rojo is the missing piece of the defensive backfield puzzle that will push the Wolverines back into national title contention next season. Without Rojo, they say, all is lost.

I have called Muskegon High School several times this season, and left messages that I am seeking an interview with Ronald Johnson, but to no avail. I refrain from calling his home directly, as this just seems like a little bit too much for a kid his age, for an interview that, no disrespect to Rojo intended, may leave something to be desired. Kids his age, I've found, usually just mimic their NFL heroes in interviews—having heard so many ESPN sound bites in their life that it's hard to differentiate a real thought from a rehashed one. So for now I trade e-mails with my sources, and settle in to watch "The Video," which is tearing through cyberspace at an alarming rate.

To: Beeg
From: Ted
Re: Rojo Video

Guys,
I'm watching the Rojo video right now . . . this is insane. What a surreal scene . . . you couldn't have written it more vividly. This has tragedy written all over it for some reason . . . I just have a bad feeling about all of it. Anyway, I'm calling the school this morning, to see what the plan is for tomorrow. I'll let you know . . .
—Ted

To: Ted
From: Beeg
Re: Rojo Video

Ted, I love the Judge, the Grandmother, all of it. The coach looks like he is tired of dealing with it. Could you imagine Lloyd (Carr) who may be in his last year, has this kid as his shutdown corner for a national title run, and he has to combat THIS?
—Beeg

To call the video surreal does not begin to do it justice. Set in a small church, Rojo is resplendent in a black pin-striped suit, and seated on the dais in a chair normally occupied by the pastor. Rojo looks a little bored, a staple of the extremely athletic, but nevertheless cuts a formidable figure. There is a large wooden cross over his right shoulder. On a table in front of a lectern—typically the place where the communion sacraments are placed—there are laid out the aforementioned college T-shirts.

First, a very tired-looking Muskegon High head coach Tony Annese ascends the dais and thanks Rojo for bringing pride to the school, being a pleasure to his coach on and off the field, setting a fine example, etc. It is the usual stuff, but I think for what should be a happy moment Annese looks a little glum. He has been through a lot. The Big Reds have won two State titles under Annese, in 2004 and 2006, and Annese was named this year's Detroit Lions High School Coach of the Year.

"I don't know what the rest of the country has to offer but it's hard to imagine a better all-around athlete in the country," said Annese of Rojo, previously, in a Scout.com interview.

"I want to say that I love you like a son and I wish you well," Annese says on the podium. "Any decision you make we're in your corner, and anything we can do to help you down the road we'll do so. We love you and thanks for sharing part of your life with us."

Perhaps the most explosive portion of the program comes next, via one Betty Rodriguez, Rojo's grandmother. She settles in behind the podium and has either spoken publicly before or is just incredibly comfortable doing so. She is a not-unattractive woman of middle age. "Praise the Lord!" she says, and when the response doesn't meet her expectations says, "Praise the Lord again!"

She then channels the apostle Paul and greets us in the name of the Lord Jesus Christ. She praises God, she says, for one of her seventeen grandchildren.

"Look how God does things, God knows how to do everything," she says, of a Rojo "who didn't even know what to do with the ball when he was a toddler." The "hook up" between Rojo's parents was, she says, from "on high." "We can't stop God's plans," she says. "We might want to stop it but we can't stop it."

This is met with much reaction from the crowd. Mostly shouts and amens and that sort of thing.

"The Lord spoke to me and said, 'I want you to tell them that whoever the coach is from whatever school he chooses will be a blessed coach and that school will be a blessed school and I will take it to the next level. Because what they have coming from them is a gift from God . . . ' "

Good to know that the Lord, in addition to redeeming the world from sin, still has time to take certain coaches and schools to the "next level." Somewhere Martin Luther is turning over in his grave.

"I know that whoever it is that he chooses, is going to be blessed. It reminded me of Moses when he was crossing the Red Sea . . . I want my grandson to know one thing: It's not all about playing the football, it's about the one who already scored a touchdown in your life!"

More amens. "And an education without salvation is damnation," she adds. Amen again. I can already tell that we will miss Betty Rodriguez throughout the remainder of the program. And I start, at this point, to feel something like sorrow for Ronald Johnson, realizing that like most events like this, the event is more about everyone else than it is about him. He, in his new pin-striped suit, is the conduit through which other people are made to feel special. Regardless of what he does, from this point forward, it will probably fail to meet these divine expectations. Being compared to Moses crossing the Red Sea is heady stuff—even if you do run a 4.4.

Next, a Muskegon judge named Greg Pittman is introduced.

"I did not expect to be a part of the actual program," he says, probably truly not expecting there to be an actual program. He seems to have retained some sense of perspective on the whole affair. Pittman expresses his admiration for the family. "This has not been an easy situation, and much has flown over and about this situation that had no business being out there," he says, acknowledging the weirdness of Rojo's recruitment. "But they have stayed above the fray . . . he is capable, he is able, and he's going to make us very proud. Ronald, I love you, I appreciate you, and I wish you all of God's best blessings."

Ronald's father takes the podium following Pittman's remarks, which were by far the most thoughtful of the afternoon. His father talks about how unbelievable it is to be here, after watching so much footage of other fathers standing with other athletes, holding up jerseys at the NFL draft, etc. He then, oddly, equates his son to a lottery ticket, an analogy which makes me, and I'm sure everyone else in the room, cringe for all of the obvious reasons: "I'm still shocked, I mean, it's like hitting the lottery . . . you just got hooked up with a three million dollar lottery ticket." Wince. He [Rojo] looks just like me, says the father, probably three times in all. He thanks God for his son. "I guess going to church does pay off," he says, finally, a statement that will make theologians cringe around the world. I feel for him. It's a nasty world, and I really hope I haven't dealt with him nastily. This is all very touchy stuff.

He is then given a "special award" by somebody at the *Muskegon Chronicle*. Johnson was recently listed as a *Parade* magazine All-American, among the twenty or so best players in the country. He is thanked for the memories, including a state championship.

Johnson then ascends the dais, and begins reading from a prepared statement. He is soft-spoken at first, needing to nudge closer to the microphone to be heard, and then, as his confidence builds, begins to sound like the athletes he has heard in a million sound bites, for eighteen years. In an endearing moment of honesty, asks the assembled congregation to "keep me in your prayers" as though he knows that the coming years won't be as easy as some would expect.

"The decision wasn't easy to make," he says, before thanking each of the schools that recruited him. "They have much to offer and it would be an honor to attend all the schools. Please know that I have strived to be honest and fair through the whole process. I know that a lot of you might not like my choice but it was the best choice I could make *[pause for clapping and amens from the crowd]*. Please respect it *[more amens, this time some screaming]*. So after much prayer and help from my family I have decided to continue my education and football career . . ."

He lets the comment hang in the air, building the necessary false sense of suspense that we have seen so many weeknights before on reality television. This is where Fox television would have Ryan Seacrest cut to commercial.

At this point Rojo's brother approaches the communion table upon which has been laid the T-shirts. Rojo's brother makes a flourish with his hand over the T-shirts in much the same way one of Barker's Beauties might on *The Price Is Right*. It is a sub-limely funny gesture and is, I've decided, my favorite part of the whole proceeding. Silently the first T-shirt, Michigan State, is placed in front of Rojo and then summarily tossed to the side. Ditto for an Ohio State T-shirt. At this point nobody is surprised, as these schools were regarded as lowest on the Rojo totem pole. A maize Michigan T-shirt is then placed in front of the pin-striped suit, and held there for longer than a moment before being tossed to the side. I can't help, at this point, but mention again that these proceedings have fluctuated from "Southern televangelist" to *Deal or No Deal* in a matter of minutes.

Finally a maroon USC shirt is placed in front of Rojo, who holds it there while flashbulbs pop and cheering ensues. They are, of course, cheering the man and his accomplishments more than the college choice. For good measure Rojo adds a USC hat to the ensemble. He pulls it down, so as to obscure his eyes as is fashionable.

Finally, the player's mother takes her place behind the microphone. Not expecting much, I zone out a little bit, awash in phrases like "thank God for the opportunity" and "I never thought I would be here." But then she does something unusual: "I want to take time to thank Michigan State University Coach Dantonio, U of M coach Lloyd Carr, Ohio State coach Tressell, Southern Cal coach Pete Carroll, and Florida coach Urban Meyer for even considering my son. I thank them for the potential they saw in him, and for taking the time to even look at him, because they didn't have to look his way."

CHAPTER 12

THE BIG BROTHER:
DAN BAZUIN, CENTRAL MICHIGAN, ALL-AMERICAN

I CAN TELL HE'S BEING sincere when he looks me in the eye while giving an answer. When he looks out the press box window, or down at his playbook, or begins fidgeting with his boots, I can tell that I will get "football answer" or "PR answer." You know, the "one day at a time, give all the credit to my teammates" type of stuff.

Dan Bazuin is a big guy, at 6-foot-4, 270, but not freakishly big. He's a big guy who got big the right ways—eating, lifting weights, and working on his family's farm in McBain, Michigan (population 597). As I type this, I realize how cliche that last sentence sounds, but Dan Bazuin is that kind of kid.

He shows up to our interview in a pair of faded blue jeans, a Ducks Unlimited cap and an old Central Michigan Football T-shirt. He has his playbook underneath one arm. It's a big black binder with BAZUIN, 93, written on the front. There is no pretense to this kid. No bling-bling. No tats. No fawning hangers-on.

"He's a pretty quiet kid," warns CMU PR director Scott Rex, who, unlike many of his colleagues at other universities is both courteous and helpful. "It may take a while to get him out of his shell."

Bazuin is a preseason All-American this season, having set MAC records in sacks in a career, and sacks in a season, last year. He is on the watch list for the Bednarik Award, the Nagurski Trophy, the Lombardi Award, and the Hendricks Award, as well as the Lott Trophy given to a defensive player who also excels in the classroom and community. He will finish his career with 261 tackles and an incredible 60 for losses to go with 35 sacks.

When I catch up with Bazuin he is fresh off an Akron game in which he was held sackless, seeing double- and triple-teams on most plays. Head Coach Brian Kelley sent videotape of thirty-seven plays into the MAC offices for their review, in which he asserts that Bazuin was either held, chop-blocked, or both.

"It's the first time I've ever seen him show frustration," says Rex, as we step off the press elevator into a nicely appointed press box that looks just like a miniature version of the ones you see in the Big Ten or the SEC. The plan is to visit with Bazuin here for a while, and then head down to field level to watch him practice.

Last season Bazuin began garnering the attention of NFL personnel as well. He has already been invited to play in the 2007 East/West Shrine game, and NFL scouts are regular attendees at CMU practices and games. They show up dressed head to toe in officially licensed NFL apparel, and skulk around the outskirts of practices, comparing notes on local hotels and restaurants because, more than anything else, scouts travel.

"I realized early on in my freshman year, when I was being redshirted, that I could play at the next level," he says. "We had some guys hurt so I got to fill in as a scout-teamer at D-line. I got to play against a guy on the first team who was all-MAC the year before. I thought if I can do this against an All-MAC player in practice, why can't I do it in a game, and why can't I do it every play? That's when I knew I had a chance to be something special in this league and then at the next level.

"Oh yeah, my parents have contemplated changing their home number because of all the calls they're getting," he says. "For me, I don't mind the mail, but I've got a lot of agents calling me and if I don't recognize the number on the phone I don't answer it. They always want to introduce themselves and their company, and talk about all the great things they've done. I'd rather just wait till the end of the season and not have to think about it now.

"One thing I've already looked for in an agent is . . . a respectable person. Somebody who isn't going to contact me during this season because he knows I'm committed to what I'm doing on the football field. Somebody who realizes I have a job to do right now."

I can tell that Bazuin is taking a good bit of solace in his job, having lost his brother Darin earlier in the year to what has been reported as a suicide. Darin won the Division 3 state championship in the discus just days before and was on his way to competing in track-and-field at Saginaw Valley State University.

"He said in his MySpace account that coming to watch me play at Central was one of his favorite things to do," said Bazuin in an interview with the Mt. Pleasant *Morning Sun*.

"It's been real difficult to get back to playing football," Bazuin told the *Morning Sun*. "The days leading up the first game [against Boston College] were really hard. I had a lot of memories of Darin going on in my head."

Bazuin has seen his football family rally around him as well, drawing support from best friend and starting MLB Doug Kress.

He was also made a team captain by head coach Brian Kelley, who said there wasn't "a *C* big enough" for Dan Bazuin's jersey.

I ask Bazuin if life has gotten, in some ways, back to normal with the rigors of football season and academics monopolizing the bulk of his time.

"I guess life for me is just like any other college student except for the fact that you go from one thing to another, to another, and you have to give 100 percent in every aspect of your life. When you're doing your academics you have to be completely focused on that. And then starting at 12:30 I have to be completely tuned in to football."

He has become something of a celebrity in Mid-Northern Michigan, a region devoid of large cities. Bazuin, along with OT Joe Staley, is perhaps the most nationally celebrated player to come out of Central Michigan, at least in recent memory.

"It hasn't gotten too bad. Sometimes I have people come up to me and say, 'Great game.' People who I may not recognize, or I may not know their own name.

"The one thing I do like is after the football games I come out and meet my family and some friends from back home. It is a great feeling. You don't see yourself as the kind of person they would want an autograph from. But through their eyes you're somebody special.

"My parents have had the greatest influence on me. I grew up on a farm in Northern Michigan. They depended on me to do a lot of chores. With it being a family farm my dad expected a lot out of me. He expected me to do my job and do it the right way. You lose part of your herd—calves and cows—if you don't do it the right way. He developed my attention to detail and work ethic."

I take a moment to envision Bazuin moving to a city like New York or Miami, and am reminded of these "small-town guy thrust into the big city spotlight" stories from years gone by—situations where you can literally watch a player, like Terry Bradshaw, grow up and become jaded right before your eyes.

"There will be some homesickness," he says, pausing. I take the opportunity to tell Bazuin about my small-town experiences, as he gets quiet. The desire, in your early twenties, to get out of the small town. And then the desire to later return.

"I'll definitely miss McBain," he says. "But at this point I'm willing to accept wherever I go. Whether it's for a few years or several years. I'm willing to accept whichever team is going to take me."

Any favorites in particular?

"To stay close to home, Green Bay would be a great place with a rich tradition. I have some teammates in Cincinnati. Even the Bears with their great defense and tradition—it would be hard not to be excited about a place like that."

Practice time is approaching, and I find myself getting a little excited. I still very much enjoy watching elite athletes practice, and actually enjoy this experience much more than covering games. I explain to Bazuin that as a college athlete, even before practice, I used to get violently nervous. I ask him if this is something he can relate to.

"I don't get real nervous. I think I prepare enough that I don't have to get nervous before a contest. I feel if you prepare enough you should know you're going to do well in a game. I know I've prepared through the week . . . and through preseason and the off-season."

I then ask Bazuin something I ask nearly every athlete I interview—whether it is winning or losing that provides the stronger feeling. Basically, are losses harder than wins are pleasurable?

"In this sport, after a loss, you're able to move on because you have a game the next week. You can put the losses behind you and move on to the next week. But winning is just a great feeling. It gives you a lot of pride and it carries you through a lot of tough practices and moments in your career."

True to form, for an ESPN Thursday night MAC game, it is pour-ing down rain and freezing cold as I wheel my car through a throng of good-natured partying Chippewas on the CMU campus. College stu-dents have blissfully low regard for people in cars, which, in fact, is something I miss about college. For a very short time, the world is your oyster. You are in control of something—your future, your education, or in this case the copious amounts of cheap beer in your trunk.

After finally making my way to the media lot, I walk right in the front gate, down a ramp past the Army Reservists who let off a cannon after every touchdown, and right down to field level where the rap/rock throbbing out of the gigantic on-field speakers is deafening.

In what has become a tradition, I phone my dad from field level. It isn't a real football game without him—it's just work.

The skill-position players—the running backs, quarterbacks, wide receivers, and defensive backs—have taken the field first. They maneuver their lithe, athletic frames around the field, plucking footballs out of the sky with ease. The level of athleti-cism, even at this level, is startling.

Proof of the emergence of the CMU football program is all around. The players' pants, jerseys, and shoes are all emblazoned with the NEW BALANCE logo, as head coach Brian Kelley secured a contract with the company to outfit the team in its maroon and gold uniforms.

"We were with Nike before," says Rex, "but we basically got their leftovers."

The playing surface at Kelley-Shorts stadium is Field Turf—the new "grassy turf" that looks and plays like grass, but has the television and budget friendliness of artificial turf. And the sta-dium sits adjacent to a brand-new, state-of-the-art indoor training facility. A recruiting standard, in this day and age.

Following the skill warm-ups, the players make a human tun-nel in the North end zone space leading out of the CMU locker room. Through the tunnel charge the offensive and defensive linemen, to shouts of encouragement.

Bazuin, to the naked eye, doesn't look much different than his defensive line mates. There are others with more girth, or with sprinter's frames. But Bazuin, to his credit, looks to be a real 270 pounds—not a 250-pounder with a beefed-up roster entry as is common at this level.

I sidle up to a middle-age man who looks vaguely familiar, dressed head to toe in New York Jets regalia. We are both watching Bazuin charge through pregame warm-ups. The Chippewas are buzzed—they bring to the game an undefeated record, and played tough in their two big-time, major conference tests against the universities of Michigan and Kentucky. Bazuin even notched a sack in the UM game, matched up against all-world left tackle and consensus first-round pick Jake Young.

"What do you think of Dan Bazuin?" I ask Jets Jacket, figuring him for a scout.

"I don't talk about players," he replies.

Undaunted, I wait a few moments and then forge ahead, hungry for a nugget of information as to where he might end up in the draft.

"I don't talk about players," says Jets Jacket again. "Haven't for twenty-five years and I'm not going to start now."

I am amazed at how the scouts still guard this player information as though they are protecting lethal nuclear secrets. The fact of the matter is that this information, and more, is all readily available on the Internet, along with film clips and anecdotes on the player's Wonderlic scores, favorite color, and fondest childhood memories—all with the intent of helping one to project that player's effectiveness at the all-important Next Level.

Jets Jacket, it should be revealed, ends up being Terry Bradway, the former Jets GM, who is actually quite friendly.

"I'm only on the road Tuesday to Friday," he says. "My son

plays at Villanova so I get the chance to see him play every week-end. It's not bad."

He is joined after a few moments by a scout in Ravens regalia (NFL Equipment gloves, toque, jacket, and turtleneck) and later a similarly dressed Bills scout. The scouts quickly huddle up to exchange greetings. One gets the feeling they see each other often on the road.

The press box offers a perfect view of the geography of Mt. Pleasant, Michigan. Illuminated in the night sky, there is a Wal-Mart, a Subway, a Fashion Bug, a Dunhams, and a Fazolis on the horizon.

While the Central Michigan stands are nearly full, there look to be about twenty brave Bowling Green fans huddled in their or-ange jackets in the East stands. I settle into the first row of the press box, next to a kid who writes for the Bowling Green student newspaper. Tonight, I learn, is his first assignment. He is en-grossed in a game of video pinball on his computer. His cell phone chirps periodically.

"Hey, I'm in the press box!" he says. "Yeah . . . I'm in the press box. Yep. Central Michigan. The press box . . ."

Central opens the game with a 44-yard run by Ontario Sneed. Later, Bazuin fights through a double-team and makes a key stop on a goal-line stand in the first half. The roomful of televisions zeros in on him walking back to the huddle after the play. Bazuin suffered a deep knee contusion and laceration against Kentucky and looks to be wincing a bit as he walks it off.

The scouts, all seated in a row behind me, are peering at him through their field glasses. They look like hunters tracking their quarry.

"It looks like he's gimping a little bit," says one, to another. "He's hobbling . . . not walking very good."

Bazuin had a 33-yard fumble return for a touchdown versus Toledo, and was named MAC player of the week for his per-formance two weeks previous. However, the injury kept him out of the matchup versus Kentucky—a game I know he was eagerly anticipating.

Bazuin hasn't gotten close to the quarterback yet this evening, but has made several key plays—staying home and blowing up a screen play, and often holding his own against the double-teams that Bowling Green sends after him on almost every play. There is a student section in the South end zone in matching gold T-shirts and sombreros. They call themselves "The Bazuin Line."

I look back over my shoulder after the screen pass in the second quarter, hoping the scouts are noticing his effort. Their field glasses are gone, and they are deeply engrossed in a conversation with each other regarding local hotels.

"I'm in the downtown Marriot in Lansing," says one.

"That's a nice place, I stayed there last year," another adds. "I'm right across the street. I'm in Ann Arbor tomorrow. You, know, if I were in Lansing I think I'd bail right now. You've got an hour drive."

With that, two of the scouts leave, apparently having seen all they needed to see.

"Yep. The press box . . . Central Michigan . . . I'm up here behind glass . . . yep, it's warm."

The chilly conditions and empty stadium (the students have since left) haven't dampened the young reporter's enthusiasm.

Central Michigan offensive Tackle Joe Staley, a 6-foot-6 310-pound Greek god of a left tackle, is also a potential first-round draft choice. Staley came to Central as a 210-pound tight end and high school track star. He has retained his 4.7 40 time, astonishingly fast for a man of his dimensions. Staley has struggled a bit tonight, and is smoked on an inside move in the third quarter; however, neither of the remaining scouts have noticed, as they are deeply engrossed in war stories. The war story is the distinct privilege of the old football guy, and must provide a sort of balm for the long, uncomfortable nights spent on the road.

"I played in the 19 . . . Rose Bowl . . . against . . ."

"I brought in Thurman Thomas . . . that was my decision . . . I believe in J. P. Losman . . . I think he has the tools . . . I coached against . . . in the Super Bowl in 1993 . . ."

And so on and so forth. Eavesdropping on these stories is not un-interesting. The men talk long into the night, breaking nearly every unwritten rule of press box etiquette. However, in the also unwritten pecking order in the press box, scouts occupy a higher place on the football food chain than the people who write about it.

After a scoreless third quarter, the Chippewas take ownership of the fourth, when quarterback Dan LeFevour—a freshman who may be the next great MAC quarterbacking product—connects with Obed Cetoute for an 88-yard touchdown.

Central Michigan later blocks a 24-yard field-goal try and then drives 80 yards to score when LeFevour hooks up with Justin Gardner for a 15-yard touchdown pass. I am especially pleased to see Gardner score, as I played minor league football with his brother Eric the year before.

Sneed finishes with ten carries for 121 yards, while LeFevour completes fifteen of twenty-five passes for 212 yards with no interceptions. And Bazuin finally tosses aside an offensive tackle, and chases down the Bowling Green quarterback, recording his first sack of the evening. The scouts are nowhere to be found.

After the game I am herded onto another small elevator and whisked downstairs, where we will walk across the street to the indoor practice facility, which will house the postgame press conference. I arrive a couple of minutes early, and walk through a facility that gleams with perpetual cleanliness. The weight room, traditionally a bastion of the strong, but slovenly, is immaculate. You could eat off the floor. I walk past photos of All-

Americans to an indoor track, complete with the latest in speed training paraphernalia.

I join the rest of the media in a small classroom with maroon plastic chairs situated around a plastic backdrop bearing the CMU logo. The players are led in—Obed Cetoute and another WR. Both players still have their game pants and Under Armour shirts on. Bazuin, who I was told would be present, is nowhere to be found.

I exit the building and make my way back across the parking lot to a rapidly emptying stadium, where I am allowed to walk right down on to the field. A handful of CMU players, including Bazuin, are still in uniform and are down on the field chatting with their friends and families. Joe Staley, the big offensive tackle with first-round measurables, is talking with a television reporter, while some of his teammates, already showered and dressed, leave the locker room with bags of ice saran-wrapped around wounded knees and ankles. Some leave with parents, a few lucky ones with college girlfriends, and most leave alone.

I see two parents standing at the back of a group of fans, their jackets emblazoned with BAZUIN, 93, on the back. They are watching their son sign autographs for kids, and pose for pictures with other CMU students. I ask Ted Bazuin if the pressure of agents calling and the high expectations has impacted their enjoyment of Dan's senior season.

"Not really," he says. "We knew there would be pressure and we knew he would see double-teams."

Bazuin sees me, and although we haven't talked since our interview several weeks before, he gives me a pat on the back and the traditional athlete hug. I congratulate him on a great game, pointing out a couple of plays where he stood his ground, fought through double-teams, and stayed in position. I also told him about the row of scouts seated behind me in the press box.

"Really?" he says, genuinely surprised. "Cool."

I wish Bazuin well and leave him to return to the duty of

being a college football hero. I resist the urge to tell him that it may never be more fun than it is right now.

CHAPTER 13

THE FREE AGENT:
HERB HAYGOOD, MICHIGAN STATE

THERE ARE A FEW minutes remaining before practice, and already Herb Haygood is tense. A former Michigan State University star, Haygood coaches the wide receivers at NCAA Division III Olivet College (Michigan). The Olivet Comets are preparing for a Saturday showdown with Elmhurst (Illinois) College Bluejays, who will bring an unblemished 2–0 record into the Cutler Athletic Complex.

A large group of players has congregated just outside the North end zone, and have gathered in a circle. The players are clad in mismatched practice jerseys, and some seem to have forgotten their jerseys altogether, a fact that irks Haygood to no end. The players seem to be chanting "do it!" as one of them has picked up and is threatening to eat a wriggling earthworm, sent upward after a recent rainstorm. The chants end in laughter and applause, as the earthworm meets its untimely end in the mouth of a pudgy defensive tackle.

"See what I deal with?" says Haygood, shaking his head. Though he was a wide receiver with stints in the National Football League, NFL Europe, the Canadian Football league, and the Arena Football league, he is still considerably larger and more imposing looking than even the Olivet linemen, most of who carry their pounds around the midsection. I am shocked at how small, and how young, the players look. And how unself-possessed. You wouldn't see the worm trick at Texas or Michigan, where a player's practice experience is planned and regimented down to the half-second, just like every other aspect of his life.

"The big thing is that this is a smaller school. There are fewer things you can get away with here. As soon as a player does something the coaches find out about it. The key is that there are no scholarships, so you have to coach the kids a little different . . . but I don't coach them differently."

I ask Haygood if there is a greater emphasis on academics here, as opposed to a Michigan State.

"Absolutely. Kids are basically here because they want to play, whereas at an MSU there are a certain number of scholarship guys that are just happy to be on the team. But on the other hand, you can always motivate a guy by threatening to take away his scholarship. So you have to find other ways to motivate guys at this level.

"I want to get coaching experience developing these guys that the majority of the football world has written off."

"Our kids think Herb is an S.O.B," adds head coach Dominic Livedoti, a former Olivet College Hall of Famer as a wide receiver. "Livo" as he is called here, is in his mid-fifties, and wears a colorful pair of retro tennis shoes on the practice field. For this, he takes a good bit of grief.

"Herb will chew your butt out if you're not doing what you're supposed to do," Livo explains. "We were lucky to get him—it was one of those 'right place at the right time' situations—and the kids are at a huge advantage being coached by a guy like Herb who has played at such a high level."

From Livo I learn that roughly 99 percent of Olivet's football players who stick with the program for four years graduate with degrees. By comparison, according to a September 2006 MSNBC article, the University of Texas program graduates 40 percent of its players.

"Division III is not leftover football, as some people put it," he says, gesturing toward his squad as they begin to assemble in their red helmets on the field. "It's not a scholarship system, so I can just play the best kids and treat all of them like they should be treated."

After warm-ups, Haygood leads the kickoff-return portion of the practice. He is still MSU's all-time leader in kickoff return yardage, and has spent a good deal of time devising plays for this unit. The players, in shoulder pads and helmets, carry around large foam pads so that they can "get a look" without risking injury.

"I want you to take it directly up the field, behind the wedge," says Haygood to DeShaun Warren, a senior DB from Detroit. This DeShaun looks like a DeShaun one might encounter at a Florida State or Miami—right down to the meticulously spatted shoes (for practice), the towels, wristbands, and gloves. Defensive backs and wide receivers are the best-dressed players on the field, regardless of the level of one's competition.

Warren gathers in a high floating kick and proceeds to dart directly up the sideline. From a distance, Haygood turns around and shakes his head in my direction, just before giving an earful to DeShaun Warren.

As is often the case with those lucky enough to be famous for anything, Herb Haygood is famous for one play. A slant pass that he took to the house against Notre Dame in 2000.

With under two minutes to play in their matchup with the eighteenth ranked Irish, freshman quarterback Jeff Smoker converted a fourth-and-10, hitting Haygood on a 62-yard slant that turned what appeared to be a certain loss, into a memorable 27–21 victory over Notre Dame.

He is slumped on a sofa in the office of Olivet offensive coordinator Bob Kubiak. Haygood, as is the case with most great athletes, has an almost bored, sleepy demeanor, but is glad to talk about his past exploits.

"My biggest play was a play I didn't actually score on," he says. "My redshirt freshman year I returned a kick 67 yards against Michigan in the Big House. That was my coming-out party. As far as the play against Notre Dame we ran the same play the play before and I was open. I went back to the huddle yelling at Smoker to get me the ball. I'm just glad they had the confidence to go back to me."

Haygood was a heavily recruited high school running back in the state of Florida.

"My first time ever out of the state of Florida was my recruiting visit to Michigan State. It was also my first time flying on an airplane," he says. "It was warm when I got off the plane," he remembers. "It was unusually warm for December. The following weekend I went to Ohio State and it was freezing and snowing . . . I called Todd Grantham [at that time an MSU assistant, now with the Cleveland Browns] and asked him, 'Is it warm here all the time?' And he said, 'Yeah.' Right after that Ohio State visit I committed to Michigan State.

"When I left for Michigan State I just told my mom I was going to work. After people continued to tell me that I was good enough to go to college, I started to enjoy the work. I always thought about going to the pros. My reasoning was that I could go to Michigan and get used to playing in cold weather, rather than just staying in Florida."

I ask Haygood if the recruiting process, in Florida, is as crazy as it is often portrayed to be.

"There was a lot of mail, and there were a lot of visits," Haygood says of the interest he drew from schools like Miami and Florida State. "College coaches would come down and watch during spring ball, which we had in Florida. I knew at the end of my sophomore year, when they moved me from receiver to running back, that I could hang and play at a high level. We had a lot of kids go D-1 that year."

Haygood tore his ACL as a freshman running back at Michigan State, and was redshirted. We are interrupted by Bob Kubiak, the Olivet College offensive coordinator, who is diagramming a play (the "Arizona" cross) on a greaseboard. He asks, periodically, for Haygood's input. "I like it," he says, to Kubiak. They are immersed in the lingo of the Olivet College offensive playbook. "We could go 'Tucson,' or we could go 'Gator,' " Haygood says, finally.

"I knew in my mind that I was better than some of the guys ahead of me, and that was by far the most challenging thing I faced," Haygood says, of his injury as a freshman.

I ask him if he enjoys the coaching aspect as much as he enjoys playing. Haygood played for both Nick Saban, a taskmaster, and Bobby Williams, a player's coach, at Michigan State.

"With Nick it was my way or the highway," he says. "And once you were in his doghouse you were there for a long time. With Bobby, he was more laid back. He would give guys second chances—even guys that didn't always deserve second chances. I think I'm pretty laid back though. You think I'm laid back, Kube?"

Bob Kubiak looks up from his papers and agrees that Haygood is laid back, until practice starts.

"I find myself explaining stuff, fundamental stuff, to the kids—things that they should have learned years ago. Whereas at MSU the players come in knowing what you're talking about. Some guys have football savvy, and some don't. I have old film of my practices with the Broncos—not just of me, but of all the receivers. I show them how to run correct routes. I love taking them up to Michigan State to show them what I expect from them in terms of how to practice."

Haygood was the 144th overall pick of the 2002 NFL draft, going to the Denver Broncos. He was mired on the depth chart behind such players as Ed McCaffrey and Rod Smith, and after being cut and re-signed, he was cut again by the Broncos in 2003. He left college a semester early, three classes shy of a degree.

"I knew I could play in the NFL during my senior season," he says. "I started making plays. I was named to the All-American team. I started getting mail from agents at the house and at the football office."

Haygood had stints with the Kansas City Chiefs, Tampa Bay Buccaneers, and Indianapolis Colts, before a turn with the Scottish Claymores of NFL Europe, where he was once named player of the week for a 95-yard kickoff return and 5-catch performance. I ask him when a player, such as himself, knows that it's over.

"I don't think you ever know it's over," he says. "I tell the kids now that I'm in training. I still feel like I can play. I worked in the Broncos minicamp this summer, messing around and running routes, I felt like I could still get open and catch passes. You just have to be comfortable with your ability and have a path for what you're going to do."

Haygood says that he still communicates with a lot of agents, but not as much for himself as other players.

"If guys have questions about things like injury grievances, or anything really, they call me," he says.

I ask Haygood about the NFL draft process.

"I was expecting to go in the second or third round," he remembers. "When that didn't happen it got to the fourth round, and then the fifth round I started getting a little sad and depressed.

When the fifth round the Arizona Cardinals called me, and they had the pick after the Broncos. I hadn't ever talked to the Broncos so I was expecting to go to Arizona and was excited about being a Cardinal. But then coach Shanahan called and said, 'Would you like to be a Bronco?' I said, 'Of course I would.' "

"If I'd had someone to tell me what to expect it would have been a lot easier," he says of his first training camp experience. "It's just football. Don't go out and try to make it into more than it is.

"In college you go to practice from three o'clock to about 6:30, but in the pro's it is literally a ten-hour job," he says. "It's more hours than people think. They don't take into account all of the meeting time, and all of the film time."

One of Haygood's college contemporaries, Charles Rogers, a former first-round draft choice of the Detroit Lions has floundered in his pro career, and is currently out of football. I ask Haygood about the biggest predicators of success on the pro level.

"In Chuck's situation I think he just got injured," he says. "I'm still a Rogers fan, you have to understand. He'll be picked up by Miami before the season is out. With Chuck he started out good but then he got the collarbone injury and started to play soft a little bit. But at the end of the day you have to get lucky a little bit and land in the right situation. That first and second round—I'm sure coach would agree with me on this one—they have TIME to develop. But if you're drafted in the later rounds you have to be as good as a second or third year player."

Kubiak nods and voices his agreement from his desk, across the room. He is poring over game plans for the Elmhurst Blue Jays.

"My high point as a pro was coming off the practice squad and being put on the roster in Denver," he says. "My low point was going from being the third receiver, to getting hurt, to getting released all in the span of three weeks. I outperformed all of the receivers below me in the pre-season, and then to have them say I didn't perform up to status. That was the lowest point."

I ask Haygood if he was left to generate his own opportunities at that point, or if teams contacted him with interest in his services.

"They contacted me right away," he says. "Eleven teams. I took eleven different trips to eleven teams and took eleven physicals. That's when I knew I was hurt. The frustrating part is that you do the team workout before the physical. So the team wants to sign you, and then you do the physical. A great example is for the playoffs, the last game of the season I was getting ready to sign with Tennessee. They said I didn't even need a workout, just pass the physical and 'we'll see you at practice.' It was like this: Monday, Miami flew me down, and they wanted to sign me to their practice squad, but my agent said, 'Don't sign with Miami, sign with Tennessee for the playoffs.' The playoffs, obviously, are more money," he adds. "So I jumped on a plane and flew to Tennessee and flunked the physical."

Haygood had sustained a pinched nerve in his neck while in Denver. He finally signed with the Indianapolis Colts as a member of their practice squad.

We are interrupted several times by Olivet players who have begun to trickle in to collect their game pants, which sit in a pile on the sofa next to Haygood. The players each open the door, eye me suspiciously, and then greet their coach.

"It's always hard to go from one team you're comfortable with, and going into a new situation. When I went into Indianapolis the coaches said, 'You don't need a playbook because you're not going to play anyway.' He told me I was just there to run the other team's offense."

Haygood communicated that he appreciated head coach Tony Dungy's laid-back approach. He also remembers his interactions with All-World quarterback and endorser of products, Peyton Manning.

"He went out of his way to make sure every new player felt comfortable," he recalls. "And he knew everybody's name on the team."

I ask Haygood, who is married, how his wife handled the whole process.

"It was hard on her, especially when I was with Indianapolis," he says. "I was with them from November through the end of the season, and that whole time she was up here."

Kubiak is at the greaseboard again, diagramming a play. "The back is on a flare," says Haygood. "And for the receiver it's a high/low read between him and the shallow guy. We're calling the outside receiver a 'Z' on that. You can 'zap' that too, out of the 'Tucson Tight.'" Haygood landed the Olivet coaching job after playing a season of professional indoor football with the Battle Creek Crunch, coached by Bob Kubiak.

Haygood says that, within twelve years, he would like to be a head coach at a major college program, or an assistant with an NFL club. He sees the Olivet opportunity as a chance to learn how to motivate players.

"People don't understand how much time the players put in, in college football," he says. "A lot of people think you just run through practice and show up for the games, but it's not like that. But for me, coming from Florida to Michigan, it gives people a chance to see different parts of the country that they wouldn't be able to see if they weren't involved in football. One of the biggest things is that I keep in contact with players and coaches, they're friends. Once a Spartan, always a Spartan."

I arrive at the Cutler Athletic Complex just a few minutes before kickoff, and drive right up to the entrance of the parking lot. In the distance I can see players warming up on the field and fans trickling into the stands. The skies are gray but the temperature is deceptively warm—it's one of those days where you'll be a little too cool in a T-shirt but uncomfortably hot in a fleece or sweatshirt. I have been informed by assistant coach Bob Kubiak that there is "media parking" on-site, and that my credential will be taken care of.

At the gate, I inquire about media parking, and am met with blank looks by a nice, older couple staffing the lot. They have an "emeriti faculty" look about them. And while I am pulling two dollars out of my wallet, I hear shouting coming from the tailgate party directly to my left, where a couple of former arena football teammates—Tim Kubiak and Kevin Kramer—are gleefully breaking several Cutler Athletic Complex rules (chewing tobacco on the premises, alcohol, etc.).

"Hey! Let this guy in, he writes for ESPN.com . . . he writes books!"

The older couple welcomes me to the lot and Timmy tries to persuade me to park in a spot next to theirs that would be tight for a large motorcycle. I continue ahead and find two grassy spots marked MEDIA blocked out near a large oak tree adjacent to the stadium.

What typically happens at this point is that the journalist shows fifteen forms of identification at will-call or the MEDIA window, and is issued a credential good for entry into the third level of the press box and the postgame locker room, but not the field. He then passes a National Guard inspection bivouac where the contents of his briefcase are dumped out and rifled through by an ROTC trainee. He is only then allowed entry into the stadium.

Today, after kickoff, I wander into the stadium with Kramer and Timmy, who have made the discovery that peppermint schnapps looks a lot like water when placed inside an empty Aquafina bottle. As I approach the college girl at the gate, I begin my "I'm with the media, there should be a credential for—"

She raises a hand and waves me in without looking up from her *Intro to Family Communication* textbook. I love small-college football.

The Elmhurst Bluejays (3–0) have jumped out to an early lead by forcing turnovers on each of the Comets' first three possessions. They capitalized, on the running and throwing of 5-foot-8 quarterback Mike Lafleur, by putting up 17 early points.

Olivet (1–2) makes the score 17–3 when sophomore Kyle Zabel (Sturgis) makes a 37-yard field goal with 11:56 left before half-time. The score remains 17–3 at the break. Before halftime I wander down to the entrance to the cleat-house, in hopes of catching Herb Haygood on his way inside.

Elmhurst takes the second-half kickoff and marches down the field, scoring a touchdown in an unusual way. Mike Lafleur connects with running back David Wilharm for a 29-yard gain. On the play, an Olivet defender jars the ball loose and Elmhurst's Michael Cooley recovers the ball in the end zone for a touchdown.

On the sideline I see Haygood shouting instructions through the ear hole of DeShaun Warren's red helmet. Warren trots out into his position as the deep man on the kickoff return. He waits nonchalantly—it is important for all kick returners to appear non-chalant—as the ball makes its way out of the sky and into his arms at the 5-yard line. At that moment, Haygood's perfectly crafted plans for a "middle return" come to fruition, as Warren follows the wedge upfield and bursts through an opening that puts him behind the Elmhurst defenders. Warren then turns on his jets to outlast them to record a 95-yard kickoff return for a touchdown. Warren flips the ball to the referee and jogs off the field, where he is met in an embrace by Herb Haygood, who used to play in the NFL and is now a coach at Olivet College.

CHAPTER 14

THE WINNINGEST QUARTERBACK IN NCAA HISTORY:
CULLEN FINNERTY, GRAND VALLEY STATE UNIVERSITY

CULLEN FINNERTY'S FATHER, Tim Finnerty, is wearing receiver's gloves and carrying an official NFL football into Elite Fitness, a nondescript gym on the northwest side of Grand Rapids, Michigan. Tim comprises one-third of Cullen's entourage today—the others being his mother Maureen and his young agent, Justin VanFulpen, of Verius Sports. The entire family has a "this is the most exciting thing that's ever happened to us" look about them and Tim, especially, is reveling in the attention. He throws an arm around his son's agent.

"It's all on you, Justin—we'll see how good you are next week!" He is, of course, kidding, but only partially. As if out of habit, Van-

Fulpen, who also represents Michigan defensive end Rondell Biggs in this year's draft, rubs his neck and checks his cell phone/PDA every few minutes. Next week, of course, is the NFL draft, or the day that will determine where Cullen Finnerty will end up in life.

VanFulpen has been working to garner NFL attention for Tim Finnerty's son, who leaves Grand Valley State as not only the winningest quarterback in Division II history, but the winningest quarterback in NCAA history. Finnerty guided the Lakers to three Division II National Championships, and has not lost a football game since his sophomore year. Needless to say, this table-running success streak has left the Finnertys with no lack of confidence.

"He's heard from the Ravens, Browns, Panthers, Bills, Bears, and Saints," says Tim, who has become something of an expert on NFL quarterback personnel in the last few weeks. He rattles off recent signings (David Carr to the Panthers) and releases (Drew Henson from the Vikings) as each may play a role in his son's professional future.

VanFulpen has been in the business for just four years, and he looks as young as his anchor client. He has assembled a group of documentary filmmakers in the gym to start photography on what will be a documentary about Cullen's ascension from Division II star to, hopefully, NFL quarterback.

"Cullen is the only player, along with Steve McNair, to throw for ten thousand yards and rush for two thousand yards," he tells me, when I suggest that Cullen may still be a little bit under the radar. "He ran a 4.62 40-yard dash, which was the second-fastest among quarterbacks behind Jared Zabransky, and he did twenty-five reps on the bench. One more than Brady Quinn, and more than any player, including the linemen, at Grand Valley."

The documentarians have herded Cullen into a small aerobics room on the top floor of the facility, which has become downright hot on an unseasonably warm day. They are from an outfit that is either called "The Team LLC" or "Going Pro LLC" or "Disney" depending on who you ask, and have taken on the project as a potential fit for Fox Sports Detroit. There are three of them, and they all wear black T-shirts, jeans, and ballcaps and have that studied, intentionally disheveled look that often identifies the very artistic.

Finnerty himself cuts a large figure, despite his measurements. He disappointingly measured a shade under 6-foot-2, which has become the NFL's magic number for determining whether a quarterback is tall enough to play in the league. I am reminded by VanFulpen that a good number of vertically challenged quarterbacks have made it at the next level.

"Look at Drew Brees, Mike Vick, and Rex Grossman," he says.

Finnerty is dressed in a white spandex shirt and a pair of Grand Valley Football shorts. He looks like a guy who hasn't lost a game in three years, sporting a combination of perfect genetics, cheekbones, weight-room muscle, and off-the-charts confidence that is often seen in elite quarterbacks. He is being put through a variety of stretching and agility drills by fitness trainer Daimond Dixon, himself a former Miami Hurricane walk-on.

"Daimond [pronounced Damon] was so nervous at Cullen's Pro Day he was almost crying," says Finnerty's mother Maureen, a quiet foil to her husband's pacing intensity. "He had put so much into getting Cullen ready. He's almost like a part of our family now."

Maureen explains to me that Cullen has quarter-size blisters on each of his feet, a product of his work in Tampa with quarterback-guru and NFL veteran's veteran Steve DeBerg. DeBerg recently housed and trained Finnerty for a week, and this sort of targeted, private coaching has become an increasingly popular trend among NFL quarterbacking hopefuls. DeBerg has also trained Byron Leftwich and Rex Grossman, among others.

"The documentary people picked up the tab on DeBerg's training, which runs about $2,500 a week," says VanFulpen. "He and Cullen really made a connection, and DeBerg has agreed to go with him to minicamp to help him make the transition."

DeBerg served as an NFL quarterback coach after a seventeen-season NFL career. He is famous for becoming the oldest player, at age forty-four, to be included on a Super Bowl roster (with the Atlanta Falcons) as well as being recognized as the consummate journeyman, never spending more than sixty-four games with the same club.

"I was worried," says Maureen, "about sending my son down to train with DeBerg. I mean, I didn't know where he would stay or what he would eat. But Steve treated him like a son."

Inside the cramped, hot aerobics room, Finnerty is poised atop a small table, which is itself poised atop a ball bearing, and is meant to improve balance. The 225 pound Finnerty wobbles atop the contraption, where he has to catch a weighted medicine ball and then throw the ball back toward his trainer. The documentary guys troll around and film the drill from different angles.

"He's what I call a football player," says DeBerg on a short trailer for the film. "And not all quarterbacks are football players. Some of them are prima donnas, but he's a tough kid."

The trailer shows Finnerty showing off his three national championship trophies, bench-pressing at the GVSU Pro Day, and throwing on the field with DeBerg.

"We've only watched this about fifty-five times," says Maureen Finnerty. "I think we've probably worn a hole in the DVD."

"I would think the NFL Network would be interested in something like this," says Tim, who has wandered inside the room to get a closer look at the proceedings. It would not be a stretch to call him a "highly involved" sports father. Somewhere to the left of Marv Marinovich, but definitely to the right of laissez-faire.

Tim Finnerty, who played collegiately at Hillsdale College, is a pharmaceutical sales rep (acne medication) by day, and a football coach by night. It was his influence that helped propel the young quarterback to success.

"With Tim it was always win, win, win," says Maureen. "There was no room for crying." Maureen tells of impromptu races in the yard where Cullen and his siblings would have to balance eggs on a spoon in their mouth while running, as well as a variety of other tasks. I look at Tim, and he looks at his wife, somewhat sheepishly, as if to say, "But it's all working out isn't it?"

As with most great athletes, Finnerty's charisma is best demonstrated by watching him do what he does on the field. In addition to his aerial exploits (10,095 career pass yards), Finnerty managed 3,042 rushing yards and an astonishing 31 rushing TDs in four years as a starter, making him analogous to a small-school Mike Vick.

His grainy highlight film shows him operating out of the shotgun spread offense, often with as many as five receivers in the pattern, and his cool efficiency is as much a testimony to the effectiveness of his line as to his own ability. He is rarely challenged in the backfield, and it often looks like Finnerty is playing a video game, exploiting lost defenses for large gains down the field.

In contrast to the largely indistinguishable huge stadiums that mark the SEC and other conferences, Finnerty's exploits take place in quaint surroundings: Small fields framed by snow drifts, and a unique wooden structure called the "Youper Dome" in Northern Michigan, which is home to the NMU Wildcats.

After spending a good bit of time around scouts on the road, I am beginning to learn how to break down film of a quarterback—looking for things like pocket awareness, the ability to throw across one's body, as well as zip on difficult throws like the deep out. Finnerty exhibits all of these, and like most great athletes appears to be moving at a different speed than most of his competitors. And he shows a Favre-ian ability to thread the ball into small areas, regardless of the number of defenders who may be in the area.

The tape also features a complete game, in this case the Lakers 49–30 win over Delta State in the national semifinals. The win propelled Grand Valley into the National Championship game, played in Florence, Alabama. It would be the fourth National Championship appearance of Finnerty's career. Following a Delta State punt the Lakers needed just three plays to open the scoring, as Finnerty found Eric Fowler for 40 yards and then Terry Mitchell for a 30-yard TD reception—both of which followed a 19-yard run by one of the great running back names in college football: Astin Martin, whose parents clearly had an appreciation for exotic, high-end autos.

Finnerty found Antoine Trent for a 10-yard reception on the next series, and would find Trent again to give Grand Valley a 28–14 lead at the half.

I tried hard to find Grand Valley games that would provide some sense of drama, but many of their games were blowouts: 49–17 over Mercyhurst, 33–7 over Indianapolis, 45–7 over Northwood, and 47–17 over Northern Michigan in the aforementioned Youper Dome. And much like in video-game world, the games become less about wins and losses and more about the massive statistics one can accrue.

The Delta State game proved to be much more of the same. Finnerty fumbles once in the first half, and makes the occasional bad throw—sailing one over the head of his receiver on an out-cut in the third quarter. But by and large he looks bigger than the rest of his teammates, because he is the focal point and the hinge on which the offense turns. This, in an era of game managers and "play not to lose" quarterbacks, is refreshing to me.

Finnerty guides the Lakers on a seven-play 67-yard drive to open the third quarter, capped by an 8-yard scoring strike to freshman receiver Blake Smolen. He will finish with sixteen of thirty passes for 365 yards and 6 TDs. The 6 TDs equals his career-high, set in the regular season finale at Northern Michigan.

Ten days later he would lead the Lakers to a 17–14 victory over Northwest Missouri State, capping a twenty-eight-game win streak, and giving the exiting senior class a 52–4 overall record.

After the workout, Finnerty pads down a back staircase and pauses to whack a heavybag as he rounds the corner into the gym lobby. He smiles a little bit, as I know that he knows what I'm thinking.

"All-American breaks hand week before draft," I say, jokingly.

"Yeah, that would suck wouldn't it?" he replies, before slumping down at the table, Tim and Maureen on either side. It strikes me that Finnerty is a rare, and perhaps dying breed in our culture: The lantern-jawed, WASPy, All-American quarterback. Being this person was the apex of living twenty years ago, but now seems to have been usurped by the very smart, the very artistic, the very liberal, and the very ethnic. Being the great-looking white guy who just throws the hell out of a football doesn't carry the societal cache it once did.

Finnerty is a nice kid, quick with a smile, but like Frank Cushman in *Jerry Maguire,* he has already mastered the art of talking and not saying anything. But then again, I may be naive to expect vulnerability from a guy who hasn't lost in three years.

"I don't care where I end up," he says. "I just want to go to a team that feels like it can use me and best utilize my skills."

His life the last few weeks has been a series of private workouts in which NFL coaches and scouts fly into town to see him showcase his skills. It is these auditions that comprise the bulk of the league's interest in him as a prospect, as he wasn't invited to the NFL combine.

"Basically for the scouts it's the last chance to see you get out and move," he says. "They want to see you go through all of the passing routes, and they also want to see how athletic you are and how you move on the run."

I ask Finnerty if there have been any moments where he felt shocked to be sharing the field or talking to certain NFL coaches or executives.

"You know, it's weird in that I've really been isolated from a lot of the other quarterbacks in this draft," he says. "But when I first got down to Tampa and started working with Steve DeBerg, I was, like, 'Wow, I watched this guy on TV as a kid and now I'm working with him.' It was kind of crazy to be out on the same field as him and being trained by him.

"I didn't know what to expect down there but it was great. We would watch film for about an hour in the morning, and then spend another couple of hours out on the field. He tapes everything. He's a stickler for technique and getting a quick release on every throw. We'd go back to the house and watch that film, and then go back out onto the field for another couple of hours."

Finnerty goes on to explain that there are really no quarterbacks after whom he patterns his game. One knock on that game is that it was honed in what has become an incredibly effective but gimmicky shotgun offense, in which Finnerty spent most plays lined up several yards behind center.

"I'm not really the typical quarterback you see out there, so there's nobody I really try to resemble," he says.

Finnerty began his career at the University of Toledo, before transferring to Grand Valley State.

"It took one trip up to Grand Valley, but then it was pretty much a done deal," he says. "But I haven't really looked back. I was coming from a MAC school and transferring down to Grand Valley wasn't really a big drop-off. At all of the skill-positions, most of my Grand Valley teammates had played Division I, so we would have matched up well with anybody in the MAC. The biggest difference was the size along the offensive and defensive lines."

In a rare moment of honesty, Finnerty goes on to tell me that he will most miss "all those wins" at Grand Valley, seeming to understand the fact that what he experienced was rare.

"Winning all those games was nice, and being the big fish in the small pond is always nice at Grand Valley," he says.

"It's one of those things that crosses your mind in high school, being a standout player," he says, of the prospect of professional football. "But I really didn't seriously start thinking about it until my sophomore or junior year at Grand Valley."

It was after his junior season that VanFulpen, also a Grand Valley alum, began recruiting Finnerty.

"We had such a big target on our backs at Grand Valley," he says. "Week in and week out people were gunning for us, so staying focused week in and week out was my biggest challenge."

I ask Finnerty, who says he admires Brett Favre and Drew Brees, what it is that he enjoys most about playing quarterback, in an effort to get him to talk. I'm realizing that there is something almost two-dimensional about the ultra-successful. I recognized the same thing in Michael Jordan.

"I like having the ball in my hands on every play, and being in charge out there," he says, without pause. It is this trait, probably, which when mixed with prodigious athletic ability is the trademark of all great quarterbacks and great athletes—the ability to want the ball in one's hands when it is all on the line.

"As a parent I just hope something good happens for him," says Maureen, as we all make our way toward the exit. "But you know what? I always knew if he was out there on the field, he'd get it done."

I ask Maureen how she knew he would deliver, how she could be so sure.

"Because," she says, "we're all like that."

CHAPTER 15

THE PRO DAY:
CENTRAL MICHIGAN UNIVERSITY

THERE ARE NEARLY fifty of them, and they are congregated in a large circle near the 40-yard line. From a distance, it looks as if the group of scouts is observing something in the middle, but upon closer examination they are trying to determine an "objective" time for the 40-yard dashes they've just witnessed. These NFL scouts—most of whom have flown great distances to kneel on the 40-yard line and hand-time sprints—are hammering out times as a group.

"This is a scouts-only meeting," a writer and photographer are told as they approach. "Adios."

We leave the scouts to their scientific work of arguing 40 times. It strikes me as odd that as a freshman in high school in 1990 at the University of Wisconsin summer football camp, they possessed the technology to electronically time a 40. However, the NFL still deems it necessary—on top of the National Scouting Combine, which was supposed to make these Pro Days unnecessary—to fly their scouts all over the country to huddle in a pack at the 40-yard line with stopwatches in hand, to determine "objective" 40 times. After nearly twenty minutes, the scouts have reached a consensus, and move on to the next series of drills.

One of the cultural expectations of this group, scouts, is that you are required to see things without looking like you're seeing things. There is no dialogue between scouts during the workout. They all stand, poker-faced, while they watch college kids run, lift, jump, and otherwise try to distinguish themselves. All one can hear is the abrasive shuffling of shoes over Astroturf and the hum of overhead lighting. It's eerie.

First, the group of scouts is led down a staircase and into Central Michigan's brand-new, state-of-the-art weight room and training facility, where the athletes wait to be weighed and measured. The majority of these athletes—the ones with promise anyway—were weighed and measured a few weeks ago at the Combine. The weight room is vast and gleaming. It is silent when we enter but a few minutes before it throbbed with standard weight-room music—AC/DC and Metallica. A group of basketball players is led through the room and into the turf bay for agility work, and the players who will be weighed and measured have congregated in a corner. They gawk at the scouts, and the scouts, in turn, silently gawk at them. This, too, is weird.

The body language differs by guy. Joe Staley, a big offensive tackle who is probably the best prospect in the group, shifts his weight from foot to foot and looks nervous. This workout is of paramount importance to him, as he was unable to run at the NFL Scouting Combine due to injury. Staley was a former track star in high school, who came to college as a 210-pound TE and lifted himself into a top-flight offensive tackle. Staley was a first-team All-MAC honoree, and participated in the 2007 Senior Bowl. He surrendered only one sack the entire season and has been compared to Detroit's Ross Verba.

Drew Mormino, a squatty, strong center, stalks around in his NFL Combine-issued sweatshirt, as if to say "I've done this before." The sweatshirt is emblazoned with "OL 31." He has a skull-cap pulled down low to his eyes. Mormino had a solid college career but really distinguished himself at the North/South All-Star Classic, where he was the best lineman on the field. He was part of a Central Michigan offensive line that helped CMU rank first in the MAC in scoring and total offense. There are several NFL teams in attendance—including the Cleveland Browns and Houston Texans—who need a center desperately. Mormino, a second-team All-MAC selection, could fill a need for them. He started every game for the Chippewas during the '05 and '06 seasons and managed twenty-seven reps at 225 pounds on the bench test at the NFL Scouting Combine.

Doug Kress, an inside linebacker, looks like Ivan Drago of *Rocky IV* fame. Square jaw. Blond crew cut. Ripped body. Though he recorded 111 tackles this season, and had two INTs returned for touchdowns, he is a fringe prospect, and will be lucky to be drafted. Another fringe guy, Pacino Horne, wears a T-shirt from Chris Carter's speed school. Mike Ogle, another hopeful prospect at DE, only started his senior year at CMU and is the longest of long shots.

Finally, there is Dan Bazuin, the other elite prospect in the room. Bazuin was an All-American at defensive end, and struggled through a staph infection and the loss of his younger brother to suicide this season. He is a quiet player, and while most of the other guys nervous-talk, Bazuin loads plates on a bench press and begins to warm up on his own. The son of farmers from McBain,

Michigan, Bazuin, unlike his teammates, didn't bother to "dress big" for the occasion. While nobody would question his dedication, Bazuin almost has the look of someone who doesn't "need" this as much as the others.

The scouts huddle around what looks like a feed and grain scale, as the large men begin stepping forward. The scouts are less people and more just a collection of logo-emblazoned apparel. The Rams Jacket. The Giants Pullover. The Chiefs Hoodie. The Patriots Parka.

As Joe Staley steps off the scale, Cleveland Browns Pullover takes out a small ruler and begins measuring Staley's hand, from thumb to pinkie. He then has Staley sit on the ground and lean forward, taking other measurements that are decipherable, I guess, only to a scout. The whole thing—the weighings and so forth—has an *Amistad* feel about it, with young men being weighed, measured, and ultimately valued based on their physical stature. I wonder momentarily if this occurs to anyone else but me, though I'm sure it does.

After weights and measurements, the athletes are placed under a vertical-jump contraption that is essentially a giant pole with little slats hanging off it, which the athletes are required to jump up and hit.

"Come on, Pacino, get up there," growls CMU's "quality control" coach, a crusty old guy named Plas Presnell. Presnell is what is affectionately called a "throwback" when teams are winning, and is called "out of touch" when teams are losing. Central, it should be noted, is winning. They won the Mid American Conference this season, and followed that with a victory in the Motor City Bowl. Their coach, Brian Kelly, left the team after the season to take a job at Cincinnati. He was replaced by a youngish guy in a crew cut named Butch Jones, who is enthusiastic about the prospect of having fifty NFL personnel under his roof.

"Get a wide shot of everybody in the room," he says, pulling aside a student photographer. "I want this for our media guide." The media guide, of course, is less for the media and more a sales catalog for the strength of one's program. It is loaded, from beginning to end, with glossy photographs of "Chippewas in the NFL," "Facilities," and current CMU players.

Pacino Horne (I can only assume he is named after Al Pacino, from *Scarface*—I both do and don't hope so, if that makes any sense) finally materializes, and takes his place underneath the pole/slats contraption. As he settles in and jumps, there is a low chatter in the room that continues. However, the chatter stops and a hush descends when 6-foot-5, 307-pound Joe Staley lumbers underneath the bars. Staley is the athlete who could most help himself today. He squats down, rocks a little, and then blasts up into the air. The ground shakes a little bit when his 307 pounds crashes back down to earth. After he lands, scouts scribble notes in their notebooks and migrate, as a herd, over to the bench-press station where Dan Bazuin is ready to perform.

The players are each required to bench-press 225 pounds as many times as they can. That's two big plates on each side of the bar for those familiar with weight-room mathematics. The scouts huddle around the bench, leaving room enough only for the bar to move up and down. A jacket from the Cleveland Browns has positioned himself as the de facto "judge" of the event, counting out reps and deciding which reps will be counted and which will not. The player must lower the bar all the way to his chest, and then lock his arms out completely at the top of the rep. Bazuin's bench performance is a reflection of his personality in that it is methodical. Each rep is no faster or slower than the previous rep, and Bazuin records the best number of the day, managing twenty-five reps. Kress, who starts very quickly, rocketing the bar up off his chest for the first ten reps or so, slows considerably before finishing with twenty-one.

In the "turf bay," which is actually a full-size, 100-yard indoor practice field, a group of "other-school" players shuffle and warm up nervously. They have been standing there for the better part of the morning and will continue to stand around through the 40-yard dashes, cone drills, and broad jump until they are called upon to perform. They look decidedly more ragged than the Central bunch—dressed in mismatched T-shirts and shorts emblazoned with things like WAYNE STATE FOOTBALL and FERRIS STATE BULLDOGS. Behind a small section of yellow police tape there is a group of friends, family, and fans gathered to watch the proceedings. Occasionally the other-school players will jog around the field or toss a football, but mostly they just stand around and wait to be called upon. It must be excruciating for them.

I am struck by how boring most of this is. Scouts move from station to station saying nothing, but congregate en masse at the 40-yard line, for the timing of the 40-yard dash. There is a young scout from the New England Patriots who looks like your quintessential Ivy League, East Coast preppie—dressed in a sweater, chinos, brown leather dress shoes, and a Patriots ballcap pulled low over his eyes. He is always sitting near the front of the group, directing the drills, and I've decided that he is either a wunderkind NFL scout, destined for stardom, or his dad is an NFL owner or GM.

Bazuin, dressed like the rest of the players now in a one-piece spandex track suit, explodes out of his stance and runs a respectable 40, clocking in around 4.67 seconds. This is my unofficial time, however, as I wasn't invited into the scouts-only objectivity mixer held right after the sprints. Though he looks fast, Kress records a disappointing 5.0 by my hand, and Ogle, who seems to fight with each yard, clocks a similar time. I should mention that with the mass of scout humanity located around the 40-yard line, it is near to impossible to record what could be called an "accurate" time, as my direct sightline includes a couple of big guys in Rams Jackets, a Ravens Jacket, and an overweight Green Bay Packers scout sitting cross-legged on the Astroturf. There has to be a better way to do this.

Staley's 4.7 second 40-yard dash will be the story of the day, and will no doubt be posted on the Internet before the scouts even finish deciding on an actual number. For a man of Staley's size to cover 40 yards in that time is unheard of, as he has posted a time that is typically respectable for running backs and linebackers who weigh 80 to 100 pounds less than he does. The run will cement Staley's status as a first-round pick, as previously he was slotted to go somewhere in the late-first, early-second round area.

Blue-chip prospects like Staley and Bazuin have been training for these events for months now. Top prospects are flown, at the cost of their agents, to places in Arizona and Florida to train specifically for these events. In addition to the 40, players are put through a series of shuttle runs in which they scuttle, crablike, between cones laid out on the Astroturf with the scouts, again, huddled around the area, kneeling or cross-legged, with their stopwatches. One drill, the short shuttle, has players running back and forth between cones set ten yards apart, and the long shuttle looks more like a traditional "ladder" like you were made to run in high school basketball practices. Finally, there is the L drill in which players run and shuffle around cones set up, you guessed it, in an L pattern. This all, somehow, helps scouts determine who can play football, after already watching four years worth of film on these guys actually playing football.

A player without the benefit of off-site training is Allen Feigel, 6-foot-6, 334-pound offensive tackle from Ferris State, a Division II school located in Big Rapids, Michigan. Feigel is being put through the offensive line drill paces, against Staley and Mormino, by a coach from the Cleveland Browns. The drills are unusual, starting with deep knee bends, and progressing into a strange drill in which the coach puts his hand behind the player's head and begins pushing him around the field. Mormino and Staley, as expected, blaze through the drills; however, Feigel struggles, illustrating the difference between players who have the advantages of indoor, year-round training, and players like Feigel who just have to make due.

On footwork drills, Feigel often stumbles and falls, and he is gassed and sucking wind, while Mormino and Staley are barely breathing hard. Finally, on a one-on-one blocking drill, Mormino's hand slides up and cracks Feigel right in the jaw, drawing an audible gasp from the stoic scouts. At the end of the drill, Feigel's T-shirt is torn and hanging off his body. He looks mentally and physically defeated.

"I'm not a man of excuses," he says afterward. "But it's hard to train for something like this at Ferris. We don't have an indoor facility. There's no place for me to run. I've been running on a treadmill, and that's not really running."

I ask Feigel if he enjoyed any part of the proceedings.

"I more just wanted to get it over with," he says. "They're good guys, Drew and Joe. Good players. I admire them and admire what they've done at this level. I just want to get a tryout. I won't be satisfied until I've done that."

Finally, I ask Feigel about the left hook he took from Mormino during the drills.

"Yeah, he got me, but that's all just part of it. You can't have feelings doing this shit." A quick scan of the room and I can't help but think that nobody here has feelings anymore. At least nobody who would admit to such a thing.

Over at the defensive line drills, it's not about feelings as a Kansas City Chiefs coach (who I would later identify as former NFL All-Pro Tim Krumrie) is putting Dan Bazuin through another weird drill. Krumrie, dressed in jeans, a Chiefs T-shirt, and cowboy boots, has Bazuin locked up, and has asked him to smack away Krumrie's hands each time he puts them on Bazuin's chest. Up and down the field they walk, for minutes on end, as Bazuin begins to tire. His arms begin moving slower, as Krumrie, age forty-seven, pushes him around the field. Cheers begin to well up from the sidelines, as Bazuin's college teammates have all congregated around the drill, and are encouraging him to continue. Krumrie finally lets up and lets Bazuin out of the drill, and with no rest immediately waves Ogle onto the field for the same thing. It is, without a doubt, the single most impressive thing I have seen today, and an amazing display of what I call "old man strength." I'm always interested, in a room full of men, to find the man who has nothing really left to prove. Today, that man is Tim Krumrie. He has been an All-Pro, and is now coaching on a high level. Compared to the majority of the scouts, and the young players, he has already done all his proving.

"It's just a little something I do to see how guys compete," says Krumrie, who adds that he has been doing the drill for thirteen years. "I like to get inside their heads a little bit."

Bazuin is then taken to another section of the field, where he is put through a series of "drop" drills by a Baltimore Ravens coach, to see if he has the agility and hands to play outside linebacker at the next level. At 6-foot-4 and 270, Bazuin is the right size to play the 3-4 OLB position, and a little small to be an every-down DE in the NFL. He catches every ball.

"The drops felt good," he tells reporters after the workout. "I had just planned on improving all of my combine numbers today . . . and I'm hearing a lot of positive things about my work ethic and character." He is asked what his best-case scenario is for the draft.

"Just getting drafted at all is my best-case scenario," he says. The other reporters leave, which gives me a chance to chat with Bazuin, with whom I have kept in touch since our earlier chapter. He looks relieved to have it over, and relaxes considerably. I ask him about his most unusual interaction with a scout, and he says that the Jets had cued up a video of his ten worst plays as a college player, and asked what he did wrong on each of them.

"They want to see how you handle pressure," he says of the film, which he didn't expect to see. "And they want to know if you know defense."

Bazuin's individual performance is definitely the highlight of the workout, and things take a decidedly less exciting turn from there. Many of the scouts have dispersed.

Cullen Finnerty is throwing on the field now, to a collection of receivers from Central, as well as a hodgepodge of long shots from Wayne State and Ferris State—two smaller schools in Michigan. Finnerty, who led Grand Valley State University to Division II National Titles in 2003, 2005, and 2006, shows great mobility, rolling out of the pocket and hitting receivers in stride. Earlier in the week, Finnerty ran a 4.62-second 40-yard dash, which would make him among the fastest quarterbacks in this year's draft. Sadly, though he ended his college career as the winningest quarterback in NCAA history, most of the scouts have left, and none seem to seek him out after the workout. This is the hard part about the Pro Day workout—waiting around for a nibble of interest from scouts.

"It's tough standing around for hours, and then having to all of a sudden step up and perform," Finnerty says of the day, which dragged on until his portion at the end. Though he won Division II national titles at Grand Valley, he faces the uphill battle of garnering the attention of scouts who seem more enamored with bigger school prospects. Finnerty, who accounted for 9,488 yards and 92 TDs in his career at Grand Valley State, is undeterred and upbeat. Part of the presentation is seeming unmoved by all of this, and he does it well. He ambles over and shakes hands with a couple of young Jerry Maguire–types in suits.

Doug Kress, however, is having a different experience. Though he looked good in the short shuttle, and in a very brief linebacker drill, he is standing alone along one wall watching his roommate, Dan Bazuin, get all the attention from scouts. Kress, who definitely passes the "eyeball test," is left alone as the scouts disperse. Finally, after working up the courage, he approaches Bazuin, who is talking to a New York Jets scout.

"Let me ask you a question," he says to Jets Jacket. "How do you think the workout went for me?"

The scout is silent for a few seconds before replying: "You need to work on your speed and such." Kress is crestfallen.

"How bad was it?" he asks.

"5.02 on your last one," says Jets Jacket. Kress just thanks him and walks away. The sad thing is that Kress, an academic All-MAC selection, is a very, very good football player who probably won't have a chance to play on the next level because of a couple of stopwatch clicks. It's a hard business.

The end of the line for Kress is just the beginning for Central Michigan coach Butch Jones, who was tabbed to replace Brian Kelly after the 2006 season. Jones, who had previously spent time at CMU as an assistant coach, is reveling in the attention a successful Pro Day can bring to his program.

"It provides great momentum and exposure," he says. "It's a great lesson to the younger kids too, as they see that the success the older guys have just filters down to them." The scouts are already salivating over a floppy-haired kid named Dan LeFevour, who started for the Chippewas as a freshman this season and led the MAC's most potent offense. LeFevour, who looks barely old enough to drive, could be the next MAC quarterbacking sensation. "You see, you get a few guys drafted from your program and the Pro Day becomes a ritual for these scouts."

I ask Jones how he plans to replace the leadership provided by players like Staley, Kress, Bazuin, and Mormino.

"It's a major change to replace guys with talent like theirs," he says. "Every team has an identity, and we're still searching for ours."

Also searching for a new identity is Mike Ogle, the big defensive end, who struggled throughout the afternoon, his lack of athleticism showing. Ogle, who started all fourteen games in 2006, is looking at the end of his football career—an inevitability that happens, eventually, to all athletes at all levels of the game. Thinking I'm a scout, Ogle approaches me following the workout with a stack of DVDs in hand. They are emblazoned with MIKE OGLE #52 and contain highlight compilations from his college career. I feel for Ogle, because he reminds me so much of myself—a hardworking grinder with little of what scouts would call "upside."

"Can I give you a video?" he asks. He is sweaty from the hard defensive line workout, and has been walking the room alone, while the majority of the scouts congregate around Bazuin and Staley. Ogle finished with 60 tackles this season and ranked second on the team with 11.5 tackles for loss. The cheers for him, today, from his teammates were among the loudest at the workout. He clearly has their respect.

"I'm going to miss these guys," he says, looking around at the players that he has spent the majority of his days and hours with for the last four years. Life, for college football players, happens for the most part inside buildings like these where they lift, run, practice, and eat their meals together.

"I think it went well," Ogle says, when I ask him how his workout went. "And if this doesn't work out, there's another combine this summer." There is always another combine, and another opportunity for athletes to pay a few hundred dollars for the privilege of running and jumping in pursuit of the dream.

"I just want to keep playing," he says, before leaving me to try to find a scout who will take his highlight film home.

EPILOGUE

DRAFT DAY

MCBAIN, MICHIGAN, home of Central Michigan All-American defensive end Dan Bazuin, is exactly one hour north of the middle of nowhere. According to its Web site, McBain is home to 597 residents, many of them named Bazuin.

The draft-day party will take place at the pole barn that is usually home to Roger Bazuin & Sons Trucking Company.

"Take a left at the first blinking light once you get to McBain," says Bazuin on the phone. "It's the only light. Go about a half mile and you'll see the pole barn on the right. If you go past it the next house you'll see is my place."

I pull into McBain (sign: MCBAIN IS THE PLACE FOR BUSINESS AND FAMILY!), past family farms and finally a diner that comprises downtown (sign: McBain is "Buzzin" about Bazuin!), I go past the blinking light, and approach a gravel road that leads to the big pole barn. Roger Bazuin has wheeled an impressive array of big rigs out of the barn and into the surrounding parking lot, which has already begun to fill with friends, family, and well-wishers.

Bazuin is dressed in a pair of camouflage shorts and a white golf shirt, and stands in front of a white stretch limousine.

"We took the limo over from my parents' place," which, he explains, is the "yellow house right over there, with the barn." The limo ride must have comprised all of about 400 meters.

Today the pole barn is home to three big-screen televisions and an assortment of Dan Bazuin memorabilia. Along one wall hang Bazuin's jerseys, including a high school All-Star jersey, his CMU home and away colors, and even his sweatshirt from the NFL Scouting Combine. An adjacent table is filled with awards, including plaques for accolades ranging from "MAC Special Teams Player of the Week" to his various All-American honors. There is also a DVD of Central Michigan's Motor City Bowl victory over Middle Tennessee State, dedicated to the memory of Darin Bazuin.

"Are you staying all day?" asks a young woman who is browsing the table next to me. I ask her if she is a relative, or a friend of the family. "Just a friend," she says. "But I guess in McBain everybody is a friend of the family."

Janell Bazuin, Dan's mother, is doing her best to make sure I feel like a friend of the family. "Help yourself to sloppy joes and cookies—there's plenty," she says, gesturing to a long table filled with provisions for what will end up being the longest first-round in NFL Draft history, clocking in at just over six hours.

"I'm a nervous wreck," she says, pacing the concrete floor of the barn, going from group to group. "But I'm trying not to show it. I've been trying to tell Daniel that he might not get drafted today. We're going to be here all day but it will be a graduation party tonight. We just have to stay busy. Dan's agent said not to get sucked into the draft coverage on TV, that if we try to watch every pick we'll drive ourselves crazy."

On screen, the Detroit Lions have just drafted their fourth first-round wide receiver in five years, taking Georgia Tech wideout Calvin Johnson, who some consider to be the best player in the draft. Janell, who has become something of a draft expert herself, is incredulous.

"They're not going to pay him No. 2 overall money," she says, channeling ESPN's John Clayton. "I think they'll try to move him." Johnson exits the green room at Radio City Music Hall and ascends the dais, where he will shake the hand of Roger Goodell and pull on the Honolulu Blue Lions ballcap and jersey. This is a privilege of the super-blue chip, as only a few players are invited to New York for the draft festivities.

After the Johnson pick, the Browns select Cleveland offensive tackle Joe Thomas, followed by the Bucs selecting Clemson defensive end Gaines Adams.

"Well, I guess it won't be Tampa," Bazuin says to his girlfriend Candace, who already looks the part of an NFL wife. "But any defensive end going off the board is good for me, I guess." It is the beginning of a long, tense day for Bazuin, who tells me that he has been contacted by every team at least once in the weeks leading up to the draft.

Candace explains that she doesn't care which team it is, that the whole process is "just exciting." She is wide-eyed and breathless, and there is a "we're about to see the world" quality about the whole thing. I'm struck that pro sports and the military are the only segments of society where a day like this, a draft, decides where you will spend the next few years of your life. Candace has a kind face, like Bazuin. She chatters on about graduation, teaching opportunities, and the fact that there are more cookies if I would like them.

On-screen, however, Notre Dame quarterback Brady Quinn is in agony. He has dropped farther than anyone had anticipated, as the Browns at three, and the Vikings at seven have both passed on the quarterback, in favor of Joe Thomas and Adrian Peterson, respectively. Quinn is resplendent in an expensive suit and vest, and looks the part of the male model/All-American boy. He is the only body left in the green room, the other draftees having already donned caps and flown to press conferences in their new cities.

"He's eye candy," says Janell, "but I feel sorry for him. If I was his mom my heart would be breaking right now." Quinn sits rapt as the Miami Dolphins—the only other team in the early first round needing a quarterback—select Ohio State wide receiver Ted Ginn. Quinn mouths the words, "That's a surprise," as cameras record his every reaction. He rubs his temples. He runs his hands through meticulously gelled hair. Pundits pundit. Mel Kiper gives his opinion on ESPN. Todd McShay on the radio, Trey Wingo back in Bristol, and Mike Mayock on the NFL Network. This kid losing tens of millions to make mere millions has become a fascination of epic proportions. Quinn, eventually, is ushered out of the green room and into Commissioner Roger Goodell's "private quarters," calling to mind snifters of brandy and cigars after dinner. Finally, he concedes to an interview with Suzy Kolber, for which he is thanked profusely, as though he has just survived a natural disaster. For the record he is drafted in the 22 slot by Cleveland, who traded up to get him. He will still be a millionaire.

Bazuin, who has been busy signing autographs for children and being wished well by most of the population of McBain, expresses some concern that the Atlanta Falcons have selected another defensive end, Jamaal Anderson from Arkansas.

"They called me almost every day," he says of the Falcons. "But it might be Oakland. Their position coach was my coach at the East/West Shrine game and they were really high on me. I've heard anything from second to fourth round."

The hours tick away slowly, as most teams take the entire fifteen-minute allotment to make their first-round selections. After being welcomed, fed, and chatted with by Bazuin's family and friends, I finally say my good-byes to Dan and Candace, encouraging them to enjoy every moment. They thank me for coming, and I get back into my car for the long ride back through rural Michigan and cities like Remus and Sidney, where I pass ramshackle houses and kids on four-wheelers who probably have no idea that there is an NFL Draft, or that it is taking place today.

Earlier in the month I learned that Michigan walk-on Max Pollock has decided to return for his fifth year of eligibility, and received significant reps in their annual spring game as a backup linebacker.

And Herb Haygood, free agent wide receiver and Olivet College assistant coach, has signed with another indoor team, the Kalamazoo Xplosion, the prospect of life without playing football harder than he anticipated.

A few of Harry Henderson's clients, though none were drafted, would sign free agent deals after the draft. Running back Justin Vincent landed with the Atlanta Falcons, and wide receiver Trent Shelton with the Indianapolis Colts. At press time Henderson was still fielding offers for running back Pierre Rembert and wide receiver Dominique Zeigler.

And Cullen Finnerty, the Grand Valley State quarterback, went undrafted but found his services in high demand, fielding free-agent offers from Buffalo, Minnesota, and finally Baltimore where he would sign. He will compete with Heisman Trophy winner Troy Smith (a fifth-round choice) and Steve McNair, who in addition to Finnerty is the only other quarterback in NCAA history to throw for 10,000 yards and rush for 2,000.

Back home I settle in for the onslaught of ongoing coverage that is the NFL Draft. After spending several hours at Bazuin's, and then a two-hour drive back home, I have still made it in time to catch the end of the first round, where Bazuin's Central Michigan teammate Joe Staley, who blazed the incredible 4.7 second 40-yard dash at his Pro Day, is selected by the San Francisco 49ers.

Early in the second round, the Philadelphia Eagles select Kevin Kolb, who was my neighbor in Mobile at the Senior Bowl. This is widely considered to be a reach, as it was felt that Kolb would be available in the third, or maybe even fourth round.

The second round also brings the selection of Rutgers running back Brian Leonard by the St. Louis Rams. Leonard's roommate in Mobile, Penn State linebacker Paul Posluszny, was selected early in the second round by the Buffalo Bills. Buster Davis, the diminutive linebacker from Florida State would become an Arizona Cardinal, early in round three.

Finally, at around 8:30 P.M., after eight-and-a-half hours of Mel Kiper et al, the Chicago Bears, the team of my childhood, went on the clock. By that time in the evening the draft had become a sort of background hum, as I was reading a novel and my wife was wondering when it would all be over. Occasionally I would zero in on the hum to hear picks from my Bears and the Indianapolis Colts, my team on the side.

"Wouldn't it be cool if Bazuin went to the Bears," I tell my wife, who peeks over the top of her book as if to say, "Wouldn't it be cool if we could turn this off and resume living our life."

After the requisite moment of drama, ESPN flashes the CUR-RENT PICK graphic on screen to reveal "Dan Bazuin, Central Michigan." Shortly thereafter his highlight package plays and his picture is flashed on-screen. I imagine whoops of shouting and celebration in the pole barn in McBain, where there is plenty of food and it would have been a good night, either way.

INDEX

ABOUT THE AUTHOR

Ted Kluck is a freelance writer whose work appears regularly on ESPN.com and in the pages of *Sports Spectrum* magazine where his column, *Pro and Con*, received a national award in 2003. His books include *Facing Tyson* and *Paper Tiger*, both published by The Lyons Press. He lives in Grand Ledge, Michigan, with his wife Kristin and son Tristan.